A NEW LOOK AT INFLATION

A NEW LOOK AT INFLATION
Economic Policy in the Early 1970s

Phillip Cagan • Marten Estey • William Fellner
Gottfried Haberler • Charles E. McLure, Jr.

American Enterprise Institute for Public Policy Research
Washington, D. C.

This volume is presented within the framework of the American Enterprise Institute's research project on economic policy and inflation, William J. Fellner, project director. Participants in that project who contributed the studies in this volume are:

PHILLIP CAGAN, professor of economics at Columbia University and adjunct scholar of the American Enterprise Institute.

CHARLES E. McLURE, JR., Allyn and Gladys Cline professor of economics and finance at Rice University and adjunct scholar of the American Enterprise Institute.

GOTTFRIED HABERLER, Galen L. Stone professor of economics (emeritus), Harvard University, and resident scholar of the American Enterprise Institute.

MARTEN ESTEY, professor of management and industrial relations, The Wharton School, University of Pennsylvania, and adjunct scholar of the American Enterprise Institute.

WILLIAM J. FELLNER, Sterling professor of economics (emeritus), Yale University, and resident scholar of the American Enterprise Institute.

Domestic Affairs Study 17, September 1973

ISBN 0-8447-3113-7

Library of Congress Catalog Card Number L.C. 73-87768

Printed in United States of America

CONTENTS

PREFACE

This volume is a sequel to *Economic Policy and Inflation in the Sixties,* a collection of studies begun in 1970 and published by the American Enterprise Institute in April 1972. In addition to concerning itself with the antecedents of the problems faced in 1970-71, the first volume attempted to evaluate the policies that were adopted during the period in which our studies were being written. The present volume continues our survey and evaluation through the spring of 1973, again taking account of the antecedents that are relevant to the analysis of the more recent period.

Somewhere between the time when our first volume was published and the present, chances appeared to be good that the rate of inflation would be reduced to a very moderate level at adequate rates of resource utilization. In my appraisal, explained in the last of the five studies in this volume, this had to do with the fact that until some time in 1972 it could be hoped that expansionary policies resulting with a lag in significant overshooting would be avoided. However, perhaps mainly under the influence of strong criticism voiced by their opponents, policy makers grew impatient and adopted a course that became, after a while, one of substantial overexpansion.

By the early part of 1973 inflation flared anew, and only partly because of adverse factors—hopefully temporary ones—affecting the supply side of raw-material markets. In good part we are now confronted with the consequences of overambitious expansionary policies against which a fair number of economists, including members of our group, have been warning policy makers for several years. The dangerous tendency to overexpand demand and then to try to suppress the symptoms by methods of direct control—methods that weaken the incentive to adjust supplies to demand—seems exceedingly difficult to fight.

To me this belongs among the most disturbing experiences of recent times. However, on no matter should I speak here for the group as a whole, not even on matters regarding which I would expect similarity of views. On some of the problems discussed in the present volume the reader will be offered a fair degree of diversity of opinion, and I hope he will find this as refreshing as we did in our meetings.

I am happy to be able to note that this time Professor Gottfried Haberler has participated in our joint effort with a paper on the international aspects of the inflation problem. Professor Thomas Gale Moore, who wrote a study for our earlier volume, has been engaged in other research, partly also undertaken for the American Enterprise Institute, and he is not among the contributors to the present volume. Professors Cagan, Estey, McLure and I have contributed to both volumes.

William Fellner
Project director

1
CONTROLS AND MONETARY POLICY, 1969-1973

Phillip Cagan

Price controls were originally imposed in mid-1971. The rationale was to contain the inflation while stronger monetary and fiscal policies were to speed the recovery and restore full employment. The experience of 1971-72 convinced the general public of the effectiveness of controls, and the nation returned to them, after the brief respite of Phase III, when prices exploded in 1973. Controls are likely to remain a serious option of policy in the future.

The interpretation of recent events presented here is that the public's faith in controls is misdirected. They appeared to work earlier only because markets were slack; and they failed to stop the price explosion in early 1973, not because Phase III controls were too weak, but because the monetary authorities, lulled by confidence in the effectiveness of controls, followed an overexpansive monetary policy that pushed the economy to capacity levels of operation at top speed. The new round of straitjacket controls will not work against the resulting outbreak of demand-pull inflation, which can only be subdued by monetary restraint.

Introduction

During the first half of 1973 prices erupted in one of the strongest bursts of peacetime inflation in U.S. history. The skyrocketing prices of foods brought housewives out in angry protest. The most spectac-

1

ular increases reflected special supply conditions in basic commodities and the devaluations of the dollar, which raised the domestic prices of goods traded in world markets. Since sharp increases also occurred broadly among prices of manufactured goods, however, it was evident that the brisk expansion of aggregate demand had unleashed a new round of demand-pull inflation. These pressures cannot be quelled by price controls which merely suppress the immediate symptoms of inflation without changing the underlying demand and supply conditions.

The new outburst was a disappointing setback, to say the least, to the three-year struggle against inflation. The application of monetary restraint in 1969 precipitated a recession in 1970. Recovery was slow, and markets remained slack during 1971 and much of 1972; still evidence of progress against inflation was slow to appear. In the half decade since its onset in 1965, the inflation had built up a momentum due to continual adjustments of prices to past cost increases and anticipations of future increases. The momentum kept prices rising in the face of slack demand. Nevertheless, during 1971 and 1972, the inflation slowly subsided while business activity gradually recovered. Then, after mid-1972, as the economy approached full capacity, storm clouds appeared in tightening commodity markets. Yet monetary policy continued to support a strong business expansion, which by then had attained boom dimensions. In early 1973 the economy plunged headlong into demand-pull inflation.

The public attributed the earlier cooling of inflation to the Phase I and II controls and its resurgence to relaxation of controls under Phase III. The administration, which had sought to disengage from the labyrinth of controls by abandoning mandatory guidelines under Phase III, bowed to political expediency in mid-1973 and announced another cycle of a freeze and a follow-up program of controls. Problems of scarcity and cost-price disparities immediately arose, indicating the kind of difficulties the new program faces because the slack markets that made Phase I and II relatively innocuous have become tight. Controls presuppose that the demands and supply costs of different products maintain uniform relationships over time, so that all prices can be allowed the same increase, whereas inflationary conditions disrupt such uniformities.

Despite the inequities and inefficiencies of controls, the general public still finds them more appealing than open inflation. Until monetary policy can subdue the inflationary pressures, controls in some form are likely to straddle the economy. The danger in this prospect is that controls divert attention from monetary policy and may encourage a postponement of the restraint which is necessary to curb inflation. This was the tragic outcome of the overly expansive monetary policy under Phase II.

The nation needs to take a hard look at the real effectiveness and consequences of price controls. The assessment made here reviews the progress of anti-inflation policies since 1969, the events that led to the imposition of controls in 1971, the subsequent accomplishments of controls, and the response and contribution of monetary policy to these developments.

Progress in Curbing the Inflation before Controls

The Recession of 1970. At the end of 1968, the inflation that had begun in 1965 was still gaining strength, despite attempts to curb it with monetary restraint in 1966 and a tax surcharge in 1968. The Republican administration that took office in early 1969 committed itself to winding down the inflation. The growth in federal expenditures was pared and monetary growth was cut from a too-high 7 percent in 1968 to 3 percent in 1969. The reduction in monetary growth was particularly severe in the second half of 1969 and effectively restrained aggregate demand.

The architects of this policy realized that inflation could not be curbed without temporarily raising unemployment higher than it need be in the long run. The basic strategy was to fight inflation with a mild dose of excess productive capacity. The slowdown in business activity was to be moderate, not a full-fledged recession. Once the inflation came under control, policy could allow output to return to full capacity and thereafter would guide it along a growth path of full employment and general price stability. In the widely quoted phrase of the time, to prove embarrassingly apt later, this was to be a policy of "gradualism."

Economists had already been debating whether full employment and price stability were compatible. Some argued that an inflationary bias in the economy necessitated rising prices at high employment so that, unfortunately, only some permanent level of unemployment could maintain price stability. Others argued that in the long run the level of unemployment was not changed by the rate of inflation. But the debate did not immediately affect the policy decisions of early 1969. Consumer prices were rising by more than 6 percent a year, and the economy was operating at full capacity. Whether or not there was a long-run trade-off between unemployment and price inflation, few believed that the 1969 combination could not be

3

improved if the economy were guided through a temporary period of reduced aggregate demand.

In the execution of such an anti-inflation policy, there are bound to be errors of commission, and this was no exception. An unintended credit crunch developed in 1969 and early 1970 (repeating the experience of 1966), which raised interest rates sharply and jolted financial markets. Also, the slowdown in activity in 1970 was larger and longer than was intended or expected. In a survey of professional forecasters in the fourth quarter of 1969 the median forecast was for slower real growth but no absolute decline in real GNP for the first half of 1970 (though a slight decline in industrial production was predicted) and for stepped-up growth in the second half.[1] This forecast envisioned a rise of unemployment to only 4.4 percent. As it turned out (Table 1), real GNP declined over the year (though, after allowance for the General Motors strike in 1970-IV, it was approximately constant), and unemployment went above 6 percent, exceeding both the previously cited forecast and the 4½ to 5 percent target set by the Council of Economic Advisers in early 1970. The outcome qualified as a mild recession. By and large, however, business activity conformed to the overall strategy, contrary to widespread public skepticism during 1969 that monetary restraint would slow the economy much at all.

The main dissatisfaction with the outcome of this strategy concerned price increases, which displayed an exasperating persistence. While the administration had looked forward to a significant deceleration of inflation in 1970, little improvement could be detected during the year. By hindsight price increases did indeed reach a peak during 1970. But skeptical opinion at the time could not be convinced without dramatic signs of deceleration, and they were not in evidence. The widely publicized consumer price index (CPI) rose less rapidly during the middle months of 1970 but, by the end of the year, it again went above an annual rate of 5 percent and showed little overall deceleration from 1969. Thus a full year of business recession had yielded no clear-cut reduction in the inflation of consumer prices. Public exasperation with this situation was heightened by the fact that, while food prices rose very little during the second half of 1970, increases in the more stable nonfood prices accelerated. The more comprehensive index of prices for the private component of GNP told the same story: it continued rising at an annual rate of almost

---

[1] Forecasts of the regular panel in the quarterly survey of the Business and Economic Statistics Section of the American Statistical Association, Washington, D. C., compiled by the National Bureau of Economic Research (mimeographed).

Table 1

GNP, PRICES, COSTS, PRODUCTIVITY, AND COMPENSATION, 1968–1973

(% change from preceding quarter, seasonally adjusted annual rate)

	All Sectors		Private Sector	Private Nonfarm Sector		
	GNP	Real GNP	Price deflator (chain index)	Unit labor cost	Output per man-hour	Compensation per man-hour
1968 I	9.2	5.4	3.6	4.9	4.7	9.9
II	11.7	7.5	4.3	2.0	4.1	6.2
III	8.6	4.0	4.0	6.3	1.0	7.4
IV	7.1	2.4	4.3	7.5	1.3	8.8
1969 I	7.7	3.4	3.8	7.4	− 1.6	5.7
II	7.5	1.9	4.9	7.7	− 0.8	6.9
III	8.2	1.9	5.5	7.1	− 0.6	6.5
IV	3.1	− 2.3	5.3	10.6	− 1.6	8.8
1970 I	3.9	− 2.5	4.6	8.4	− 1.8	6.5
II	5.9	1.5	4.6	2.4	4.7	7.2
III	6.1	2.0	3.2	2.0	6.9	9.0
IV	1.4	− 4.8	5.6	8.0	− 3.1	4.6
1971 I	14.3	8.0	5.5	1.5	7.4	9.1
II	7.9	3.4	4.4	4.2	3.2	7.5
III	5.4	2.5	3.4	2.5	2.5	5.2
IV	8.3	6.7	1.4	.3	4.7	4.9
1972 I	12.0	6.5	4.4	3.8	5.2	9.1
II	11.4	9.4	2.3	−.5	5.1	4.6
III	8.9	6.3	2.9	−.4	6.6	6.1
IV	11.0	8.0	2.9	3.6	3.6	7.6
1973 I	15.2	8.0	6.8	5.8	4.3	10.4

Source: *The Annual Report of the Council of Economic Advisers,* 1972 and 1973, and U.S. Department of Commerce, *Survey of Current Business;* both publications printed by the U.S. Government Printing Office, Washington, D. C.

5 percent, practically unchanged from 1969 (Table 1). The index of wholesale industrial prices fluctuated during 1970, but over the year as a whole showed no tendency to decelerate. Its annual rate was 3½ percent for the second half of 1970, somewhat lower than earlier in the year but above the corresponding rates of mid-1969.

One encouraging sign was the behavior of consumer service prices, which had a rising rate of increase in early 1970 but a decelerating rate during the second half of the year. This was due only in part to declining mortgage interest rates (included in the services component). Nevertheless, its annual rate of increase in

December was still more than 7 percent, and its downward trend had not gone far enough to be apparent by the end of 1970.

It is not unusual, however, to make little headway against an on-going inflation during a recession. Chart 1 shows monthly rates of change and centered six-month average rates in the CPI, excluding foods, for the recent years and for the previous U.S. inflation in the late 1950s. (Although foods are an important part of the cost of living, they are subject to volatile fluctuations induced by changes in supply conditions and may be excluded in representing inflationary tendencies due mainly to aggregate demand.) [2] The inflation that began in 1954 had begun to moderate in 1956. It did not decline much during most of the recession of July 1957–April 1958 but did subside dramatically just before and after business activity started to recover. A similar phenomenon occurred in the business recovery of 1971, though not until after the cyclical trough in November 1970. The reason for the delayed effect of a recession on prices is that inflation does not decelerate on a broad front until labor costs do, and then only with a lag. Unit labor costs can be separated into compensation of workers and productivity (output per man-hour). Compensation reflects wage rates, which typically decelerate very slowly. Output per man-hour actually declined slightly during 1969 with production at full capacity, but it began to improve during the recession as businesses trimmed their work forces (thus holding down increases in unit labor costs). Prices ordinarily do not respond right away to improvements in productivity, because the first benefits of cost cutting go to bolster depressed profit margins. But, after a while, the reduced rate of increase in unit labor costs puts less upward pressure on prices. With this initial deceleration of inflation, its anticipated rate declines and contributes to a reduction of wage demands and thus to a further deceleration in costs and prices.

Although a recession does not stop inflation immediately, therefore, it initiates this deceleration in unit labor costs, which is the first stage in the process of reducing inflation and which can continue even after business begins to recover. Indeed, the business recovery contributes to the deceleration in unit labor costs—up to a point—because an expansion of production brings a greater utilization of fixed resources; this shows up as increases in output per man-hour. The lack of progress in curbing inflation during the 1970 recession did not, therefore, preclude a policy designed to foster a strong recovery in 1971.

---

[2] Such a separation between demand and supply influences is not fully possible, of course. For a given level of aggregate demand, higher expenditures on foods mean lower expenditures on other goods and services.

Chart 1

CONSUMER PRICE CHANGES (EXCLUDING FOODS) IN TWO INFLATIONARY PERIODS, 1956-60 AND 1969-73

(percent per year)

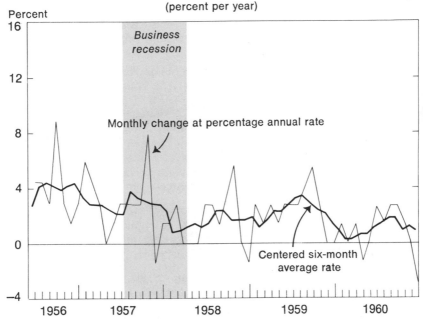

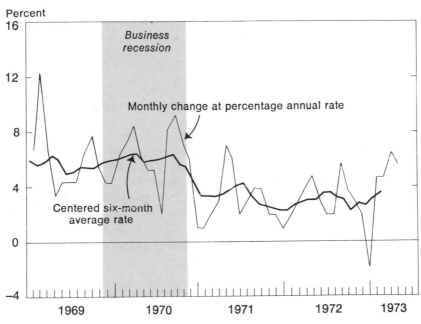

Of course, a recovery in demand would exert an upward pull on many wholesale prices, particularly on those of basic commodities. But most of these increases would taper off, as they had in 1959, if aggregate demand did not rise so much as to strain productive capacity and if unit labor costs continued to decelerate. The hoped-for business recovery would not foreclose further progress in curbing inflation.

The Business Recovery of 1971. All sights were therefore set on the business recovery forecast for 1971. Early in the year the Council of Economic Advisers (CEA) set a GNP target for 1971 of $1,065 billion, or 9.1 percent over 1970. This would have amounted to an unusually rapid recovery from a recession as mild as that of 1970. It represented a policy target as much as a forecast, since a vigorous recovery was very much desired to reduce unemployment.

Disagreement arose over how vigorously monetary policy should push the recovery. The CEA's target of a 9 percent increase in GNP for 1971 seemed to call for 7 to 8 percent or more growth in the money supply (defined as currency plus checking deposits). In his testimony to the Joint Economic Committee at the beginning of the year, Federal Reserve Board Chairman Burns viewed such a policy as too ambitious and stated that the Federal Reserve would pursue a more moderate growth target. This implied continuation of the 6 percent average monetary growth that had prevailed during most of 1970 and through January 1971.

From February until July, however, the annual growth rate spurted to 10.8 percent, once again confounding the prognosticators of monetary policy (Chart 2). For the first few months the spurt compensated for slow growth in the latter part of 1970, but that deficiency was made up by the beginning of the second quarter. What happened then was that the Federal Reserve resisted the cyclical recovery in interest rates, which began to climb sharply in March and continued rising until midyear. The yield on Treasury bills rose from 3½ to 5½ percent, and most long-term bond yields rose ½ to ¾ of a percentage point. The monetary spurt was justified by the Federal Reserve staff as necessary to supply an increased demand by the public to hold money balances. The staff's econometric estimates of the demand suggested that it had shifted upward in the second quarter. Another estimate later, however, questioned that interpretation.[3] If no shift had occurred, the sharp rise in interest rates could be attributed to the usual recovery of

---

[3] Michael J. Hamburger, "The Demand for Money in 1971: Was There a Shift?" forthcoming in *Journal of Money, Credit and Banking.*

Chart 2
MONETARY GROWTH, 1969-73
(percent per year)

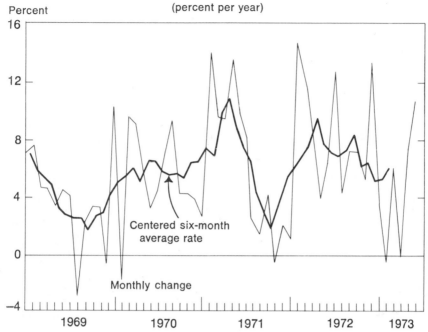

Note: Money stock is demand deposits and currency

credit demand in the first stage of a cyclical expansion. The Federal Reserve sought to slow the rise in interest rates for fear that it might go too far and impede the business recovery. But the high monetary growth resulting from this policy choice raised fears of its own for the inflation. By summer, interest rates stopped rising, mercifully in view of the Federal Reserve's continuing dilemma whether to restrain monetary growth or interest rates, and monetary growth was reduced to a 1 percent annual rate for the remainder of the year, resulting in 6.5 percent growth for all of 1971.

Despite the upturn in monetary growth during 1970 and the spurt in the first half of 1971, the business recovery started off weakly. Shallow business contractions tend to be followed by slow recoveries; even then, this one was unusually slow. Forecasts for the first year of a business upturn often underpredict the strength of a recovery, but in this case it was the private forecasts for 1971, which had been much less optimistic than the CEA's figure, that turned out to be correct. Except for the first quarter, which was pushed up by the ending of the General Motors strike, the quarterly increases in output were low. For the year as a whole, GNP rose 7.6 percent in dollar terms and only 2.7 percent in real terms. Homebuilding accounted for much of the increase. It had fallen behind the growth of households owing to the dearth of mortgage funds during the credit crunch of 1969 and early 1970. With funds now readily available, the dollar amount of residential construction rose 44 percent from 1970 to 1971. The accompanying high rate of house purchases meant that consumer expenditures would spread to home furnishings in due course, but that did not happen until 1972. Even a flurry of new automobile purchases in August, due to the removal of the excise tax, faltered after several months. Consumers were consolidating their financial position: personal saving for the year rose to the unusually high rate of 8.2 percent of disposable income, and surveys of households revealed a general disposition to spend cautiously.[4] Nonresidential business-fixed investment declined slightly. Since productive capacity remained ample to meet the increases in demand and sales trends showed little strength, businesses felt no need to expand facilities. Growth in the labor force offset the modest increases in employment, and unemployment remained around 6 percent. It did not decline even the modest 1/2 percentage point projected by most private forecasters at the beginning of the year.

Yet, productivity gained nicely during the slow recovery. The improvement was not recognized at first because, with a low fourth quarter due to the General Motors strike, output per man-hour (private nonfarm sector) grew only 1.6 percent for the calendar year. But, from the first quarter of 1970 to the second quarter of 1971, it rose 3.8 percent at an annual rate compared with a decline for 1969 (Table 1). Unit labor costs for the private nonfarm sector consequently rose only 3.6 percent per year for that period compared with 8.2 percent in 1969—even though compensation per man-hour rose 7.5 percent per year, up slightly from 6.9 percent in 1969. Because profit margins were depressed and now were being raised, how-

---

[4] In the Census Bureau survey of *Consumer Buying Expectations*, taken in July 1971, the index of expected automobile purchases for the third quarter of 1971 dropped to its lowest level in several years, and the indexes for household durables and appliances also declined sharply.

The question arises whether the high saving was in some way due to the inflation. One study claims that it was, on the grounds that *un*anticipated price increases lead to reduced expenditures and to increases (temporarily at least) in all forms of saving (including fixed-dollar assets, which anticipated inflation presumably leads people to avoid), because of fears of a decline in household real income. See F. Thomas Juster and Paul Wachtel, "A Note on Inflation and the Saving Rate," *Brookings Papers on Economic Activity*, 3: 1972 (Washington, D. C.: The Brookings Institution, 1972), pp. 765-778.

Table 2

RATE OF CHANGE IN CONSUMER PRICE INDEX
AND CONTRIBUTION OF MORTGAGE INTEREST

(centered six-month average at annual percentage rate)

	Total, Excluding Food	Contri- bution of Interest	Total, Excluding Food and Interest		Total, Excluding Food	Contri- bution of Interest	Total, Excluding Food and Interest
1969				*1970*			
Mar.	5.7	.5	5.2	Oct.	5.6	− .2	5.7
Apr.	6.3	.6	5.7	Nov.	5.4	− .4	5.7
May	5.9	.6	5.2	Dec.	4.4	− .7	5.0
June	4.9	.5	4.4	*1971*			
July	5.1	.3	4.8	Jan.	3.3	− .9	4.2
Aug.	5.4	.3	5.1	Feb.	3.3	− .9	4.3
Sep.	5.4	.3	5.1	Mar.	3.3	− 1.0	4.2
Oct.	5.4	.2	5.1	Apr.	3.5	− .8	4.3
Nov.	5.7	.4	5.3	May	3.8	− .6	4.4
Dec.	5.8	.6	5.2	June	4.1	− .2	4.3
1970				July	4.3	.0	4.2
Jan.	6.0	.6	5.4	Aug.	3.4	.1	3.3
Feb.	6.1	.6	5.6	Sep.	2.8	.1	2.7
Mar.	6.3	.5	5.8	Oct.	2.6	.1	2.5
Apr.	6.4	.5	5.9	Nov.	2.4	.0	2.4
May	5.7	.3	5.4	Dec.	2.3	− .1	2.3
June	5.8	.0	5.8	*1972*			
July	6.0	.0	6.0	Jan.	2.2	− .1	2.4
Aug.	6.1	.0	6.1	Feb.	2.7	− .1	2.8
Sep.	6.2	.0	6.2	Mar.	2.9	− .1	3.0

Notes: Total index is all items excluding food (same as series plotted in Chart 1). Contribution of mortgage interest is the rate of change of this component times each December's weight in the total index, applied from June to June of the fiscal year.

Difference between columns 1 and 2 may not exactly equal column 3 because of rounding.

ever, the deceleration in unit labor costs had little discernible effect on most prices. From the first quarter of 1970 to the second quarter of 1971, the private GNP deflator (chain index) rose 4.7 percent per year compared with 4.9 percent for 1969. The slower growth in unit labor costs was bound to affect the inflation rate sooner or later, and a delay was not unusual. But prices were decelerating more slowly than in 1958-59, presumably because inflation in 1971 had lasted longer and in various ways had become more entrenched.

Nevertheless, the inflation was subsiding, as was most clearly apparent in the consumer price index. The rate of increase in this index (excluding foods) declined during the first half of 1971 from over 6 percent per year to 3½ percent (six-month periods, Chart 1). Part of this decline, however, reflected a fall in mortgage interest, which is a cost of living for borrowers but not an indication of the purchasing power of money vis-à-vis goods and services. If mortgage interest is excluded from the index (Table 2), a peak rate of about 6 percent per year in late summer 1970 declined to 4.3 percent in the second quarter of 1971. This was a reduction of over 1½ percentage points.

The lack of uniformity in the various price indexes, however, confused the picture. Even the personal consumption component of the GNP deflator differed from the CPI, although the two covered the same general group of expenditures. The explanation was that the GNP deflator had a different weighting scheme than the CPI and used many additional series.[5] Neither one was clearly preferable. While the CPI gave a closer approximation to the purchasing power of a dollar spent by consumer households, the GNP deflator gave a more comprehensive measure of the dollar's purchasing power for all goods and services. The conflict between the CPI and the GNP deflator made the direction of inflation uncertain and created doubt that deceleration of the CPI was giving an accurate picture.

The suspicion that little lasting headway was being made against inflation found reinforcement in the wholesale price index. The industrial commodities component of this index showed no deceleration from early in 1970 to mid-1971. From March 1970 to June 1971, six-month average rates of increase deviated very little from 3¾ percent per year. In the third quarter of 1971 the index even accelerated.

The confusion over prices, the weak business recovery, and the lack of dramatic improvement in unemployment created a gloomy economic condition, and prospects for a sluggish second half pointed to more of the same. The median forecast for the second half by the experts reporting to the American Statistical Association in its early August survey was for a 7.8 percent increase in dollar GNP and only a 3 percent increase in real GNP (annual rates). (In actuality, dollar GNP rose 6.8 percent per year in the second half, while real GNP rose 4.5 percent.)

At midyear 1971, given the appearance of little progress in reducing unemployment after a year and a half of sizable growth in money, a growing number of commentators supported nonmonetary proposals to add some zip to the recovery. Proposals for price

---

[5] Most of this discrepancy was due to differing treatment of the housing sector, however. See Jack E. Triplett and Stephen M. Merchant, "The CPI and the PCE Deflator: An Econometric Analysis of Two Price Measures," *Annals of Economic and Social Measurement*, vol. 2, no. 3 (1973).

controls received the widest attention. Such controls were thought relevant to both the inflation and unemployment problem, on the assumption that the growth in dollar GNP was determined by monetary and fiscal policy and hence any reduction in inflation would allow more growth in real terms. Since 1970 Federal Reserve Chairman Burns had been pressing the Congress and the administration for direct governmental influence in wage and price setting. Like many others in the middle range of opinion, he advocated an "incomes" policy, that is, the imposition of limits on wage and price increases. Impatience with the slow progress against inflation and unemployment was building up within the administration as well.

Around midyear the recovery sagged for a few months and seemed to many to be about to expire. Industrial production, which had regained about half of its recession decline by May 1971, leveled off in June and fell slightly in July and August. Such a long pause was unsettling because it was unusual for the first stage of a cyclical recovery. Then, during the summer, foreign exchange markets acted up, forcing the administration to take action to stem speculation against the dollar. The U.S. balance of payments (as measured by the net liquidity balance) had been in deficit since the late 1950s and deteriorated further during the Vietnam War. Holders of liquid international balances were alert to the possibility of a dollar devaluation. When the traditional U.S. surplus on goods and services declined further in the second quarter of 1971—this time practically to zero— the speculative outflow became a tidal wave. In the first half of 1971, U.S. liabilities to official foreign institutions (as recorded by the U.S.) rose by $10.2 billion.

The administration might have tried the simple ploy of reasserting its determination not to seek a devaluation of the dollar but, without steps to back it up, the announcement would not have been credible. Instead it decided to institute a full-scale activist policy in order to disarm the critics who charged the anti-inflation program with failure and who called for strong medicine. Thus the administration took its first step into the thicket of direct controls which it had once vowed to avoid.

The Economy under Controls

The Administration's Economic Stabilization Program. The new program announced in the President's speech of August 15, 1971, had three basic parts: (1) It set forth steps designed to lead to a devaluation of the dollar through the appreciation of foreign currencies (the dollar was an international reserve currency to which other currencies were pegged and could not be devalued unilaterally), including a temporary surcharge of 10 percent on dutiable imports to use as a bargaining weapon in international negotiations. (2) It reduced selected taxes to stimulate the slow business recovery. (3) It froze prices and wages for ninety days (Phase I) to be followed by controlled increases for an indefinite period thereafter. (Phase II was followed by a milder Phase III in January 1973 and then by the reimposition of a freeze in June 1973.)

The devaluation had far-reaching implications for the international financial system and set off a series of discussions that is still under way on how to build a system better able to redress payment imbalances. At first the degree of dollar devaluation to occur against each currency was contested. Finally on December 18, in an international meeting at the Smithsonian Institution in Washington, an interim agreement was reached. The various foreign currencies were appreciated by different amounts, producing an average appreciation against the dollar at the end of 1971 calculated at about 8 percent for total U.S. trade. (The gold value of the dollar was also changed from $35 to $38 an ounce, which meant that the appreciation of foreign currencies against gold was less than against the dollar, but this difference was of no significance for international trade.) As part of the agreement, the U.S. import surcharges imposed on August 15 were removed, the permissible band of fluctuation in exchange rates was widened from 1 to 2¼ percent, and plans were laid for further negotiations to modify the mechanism of international financial adjustments. The devaluation was expected to improve the U.S. trade balance, though the full effect would not be felt for several years. (Little effect was in fact discernible during 1972, because the trade balance deteriorated markedly as the business recovery picked up. As a consequence, pressures against the dollar reappeared late in 1972, culminating in a further 10 percent devaluation in January 1973 and the floating of the Common Market currencies and the yen in March.)

The effects of the fiscal stimulants of the stabilization program mainly came in the final four months of 1971, but they were not of major importance for the economy at large. Except for the import surcharge, they comprised a number of proposed tax reductions designed to encourage spending, including removal of the 7 percent excise tax on automobiles and a tax credit on new investment. The CEA estimated that these proposals would reduce fiscal year 1972 revenues (excluding the surcharge) by $5.8 billion and expenditures by $4.9 billion. As finally enacted by Congress, the actual revenue reduction was estimated to be $4.6 billion. The net effect on the budget deficit was very small and could not have affected aggregate demand much either way. The main purpose was to encourage early purchases of certain domestic goods that otherwise would not have been made until later.

The wage-price controls were the most dramatic step for the domestic economy and for anti-inflation policy. They were not, to be sure, a substitute for the previous policy of maintaining aggregate demand below potential output, which was not to be abandoned. Controls were not viewed as effective against excessive demand pressures. Past experience had indicated that if controls were used to suppress excess demand, the result would be shortages, black markets, and quality deterioration as manufacturers sought to evade the price ceilings. The purpose of the controls, as implied in the 1972 *Annual Report of the Council of Economic Advisers,* was to hold down price increases made in anticipation of further inflation. While the gap between potential and actual output brought about by appropriate monetary and fiscal management had created the necessary and sufficient conditions for curbing the inflation, anticipations of inflation were leading to price and particularly wage increases inconsistent with aggregate policy. Controls were intended to hasten the deceleration in inflation through their announcement effect on anticipations.

Given the objective of influencing anticipations, an elaborate enforcement agency was not necessary and indeed was economically impractical—in addition to being politically repugnant to the administration. The idea was to do little to disrupt the economy. Controls were to prevent most of the very large union wage settlements and to force firms with "reasonable" profits to absorb some cost increases and so foster public confidence that inflation was gradually coming under control.

Thus, the ninety-day freeze was followed by a Phase II set of regulations administered by a small organization specially set up for the purpose. The key operating centers of the organization were a Price Commission of seven public members to control prices and a Pay Board of fifteen members split equally among business, labor, and public representatives to pass on wages and salaries. The Construction Industry Stabilization Committee for controlling construction wages was incorporated into the organization, and other groups were formed to advise on or deal with dividends and interest, government pay, health services, and rents. Each of these groups had a staff numbered in the hundreds. Public inquiries, complaints, and

15

general enforcement were taken on by the Internal Revenue Service, which assigned 3,000 employees to the task. In fact, very little litigation was instituted. The entire program was run to a considerable extent by voluntary compliance. And it had to be: the full-scale price control apparatus of World War II involved 60,000 paid workers and many thousands more volunteers.

The lack of a large enforcement agency meant that the controls had to be limited in scope. This was done by exempting all but large firms from direct control. The nonexempt firms comprised the so-called Tier I: for prices, the 1,500 firms with annual sales of $100 million or over (45 percent of total sales in the economy) and, for wages, labor contracts affecting 5,000 or more workers (10 percent of all employees). Tiers II and III of smaller firms had to follow the guidelines set down for price and wage increases but could act without prior approval (though Tier II firms had to give prior notification). The guidelines were 2½ percent per year for prices and 5½ percent for wages (6.2 percent including fringes), with an allowance up to 1½ percent for catching up. (The 2½-price and 5½-wage guidelines were mutually consistent under the assumption that labor productivity would rise on the average 3 percent per year.)

Initially agriculture (including fisheries and forests), exports and imports, pay scales and fees of the federal government, and interest rates were exempt. The exemption was extended, in January 1972, to retail firms with annual sales below $100,000 and to apartments of four or less units or with monthly rents above $500 and, in May, to firms and governmental units of sixty employees or less (with some exceptions).

This confinement of direct controls to large units meant that the sparse enforcement machinery could efficiently narrow its responsibility. But the policy also conformed to the popular view that the inflation originated in the aggressive policies of large corporations and large unions. Only the atomistic markets, such as those for farm and other basic commodities, apartments, and financial assets, were thought to be self-regulating. Contrary to this view, however, the impetus of the inflation was not coming from industries dominated by large corporations; indeed, the general decline in corporate profit margins during the inflation indicated that most corporations were having difficulty simply keeping up with cost increases. Whether big unions were responsible for prolonging the inflation was a more complex question. To a large extent new union contracts simply made up for increases in the cost of living since the last contract and thus were not independent sources of inflation. But many unions also used their power to outdo each other and to cover in new contracts the anticipated future increases in the cost of living. Some of the large settlements seemed to accomplish all this and more, and thus to prolong the inflation. Union leaders were not illogical to conclude that the controls were aimed primarily at union wage contracts. Labor leaders voiced their opposition but failed to dent the public support for restraining union wage demands.

To avoid a knockdown confrontation with labor, the Pay Board wielded its authority cautiously. In the initial weeks it approved large increases negotiated by several powerful unions, explaining that the increases had been previously negotiated or that the wage rates in question had fallen behind so that the increases were allowed under the catching-up or gross inequity provisions of Phase II. But the board gradually tightened its rein: In a well-publicized decision early in 1972 it pared down a settlement of the West Coast longshoremen who threatened a showdown strike but finally backed off. Overall, the increases approved through June 1972 averaged 5.1 percent for union workers and 4.4 percent for nonunion workers.[6] Flexible enforcement of wage controls succeeded in avoiding resentment. Although AFL-CIO President George Meany pulled union representatives off the Pay Board in March (whereupon the administration reorganized it with seven public members), the board was generally accepted by business, the union rank and file, and the public.

Acceptance and compliance had been uncertain when the controls were first imposed. Other Western countries, notably Great Britain, had instituted various kinds of "incomes" policies during the 1960s, but with little evidence of more than temporary success.[7] They were resisted by labor and generally broke down. The key differences between the U.S. case and the others appeared to be the slack in the U.S. economy and the fact that controls had not been used since the Korean War, so Americans had been spared a recent opportunity to become disenchanted with them.[8] Of course, 1972 was a year of reduced labor negotiations: major contracts (1,000 employees or more) affected only 2.8 million workers that year, compared with

---

[6] Barry Bosworth, "Phase II: The U.S. Experiment with an Incomes Policy," *Brookings Papers on Economic Activity*, 2: 1972 (Washington, D. C.: The Brookings Institution, 1972), Table 4.

[7] See Eric Schiff, *Incomes Policies Abroad, Part I: United Kingdom, The Netherlands, Sweden, Canada*, 1971, and *Incomes Policies Abroad, Part II: France, West Germany, Austria, Denmark*, 1972 (Washington, D. C.: American Enterprise Institute).

[8] Great Britain copied the Phase I formula in November 1972 and instituted Phase II in April 1973, but aggregate demand has remained strong, and the controls have not been notably successful in stemming continued inflation.

4.75 million in both 1970 and 1971, and 5 million to be affected in 1973.

Prices and Wages under Phase I and II. The ninety-day freeze of 1971 achieved its purpose. Although wholesale industrial prices rose at a 6.6 percent annual rate in June and July compared with a 3.8 percent rate in the preceding six months, suggesting that some firms had a premonition of what was to come, in general the freeze was not expected and a difficult-to-administer rollback of prices did not appear necessary and was not seriously contemplated. During the freeze the recorded prices of covered items did not rise and no evidence of widespread evasion came to light. Many prices rose because of exemptions (which included basic foods, imports, and seasonal variations). But others fell due to market conditions, and the overall wholesale price index was practically unchanged during the period. A special analysis of consumer prices showed little rise in covered prices during the freeze.[9] As to wage increases, with some exceptions, they were stopped.

Of course, this freeze was successful without much enforcement because there was slack in the economy, and because adjustments were to be allowed afterward, and because the economy can endure almost anything for only three months. The effect on prices if the freeze and post-freeze quarters are combined was much more modest. Right after the freeze, there were catch-up increases in prices and wages which the Phase II controls attempted to moderate but not prevent altogether. As a result, the rise in the total CPI (annual rate) jumped from 1.9 percent during the freeze to 4.8 percent during the three months following the freeze. For the six months combined the annual rate of increase was 3.4 percent, compared with 4.0 percent for the preceding six months. Allowing for the fact that the inflation had been decelerating due to reduced aggregate demand, the additional decline that could be attributed to the freeze was slight.

The post-freeze offset was not unexpected or thought undesirable by policy makers, because the controls had not been intended to cut too radically into inflation for fear of disrupting business activity. The freeze satisfied the public's clamor in mid-1971 for some dramatic new initiative against inflation and, at the same time, constituted a needed holding action while the Phase II controls were planned and

---

[9] *Annual Report of the Council of Economic Advisers,* 1972, p. 81. The freeze specified that prices could not rise above the highest level of substantial transactions (10 percent or more) in the previous thirty days or above the level of May 1970 if higher, with special provisions for seasonal or seldom-traded goods.

set up. The planning operation could not have been kept secret and, without the freeze, would have touched off a spate of anticipatory price increases.

Under Phase II inflation fell appreciably. This was not widely recognized in early 1972 because of the attention paid to price increases for exempt foods and other basic commodities. But by late summer the overall indexes showed substantial deceleration (Chart 1 and Table 1). The private deflator (chain index) rose 5 percent at an annual rate in the first half of 1971, whereas its annual rate averaged 2.6 percent in the second and third quarters of 1972 after the catch-up increases in the first quarter.

The coincidence of controls and deceleration convinced the public that controls were effective. Yet the deceleration could not have been caused solely by controls, since it had started earlier in many sectors in response to slack demand.

How much of the deceleration from mid-1971 to the end of 1972 can be attributed to controls? The initial acquiescence of the business community to the burden of operating under controls reflected a belief that only controls could stop the wage explosion. The large increases in union settlements apparently did moderate faster with the help of controls. The Construction Industry Stabilization Committee, which began operations in March 1971 before the freeze went into effect, helped to restore order to a chaotic wage structure. First-year wage increases in construction contracts, which had averaged 9 percent in 1968, started rising again in 1969, and reached 21 percent in the second half of 1970. They came down to 11 percent by the end of 1971 and to 6 percent by the end of 1972. For other workers as well, the frequency of large settlements was reduced. First-year wage increases were above 9 percent for 56 percent of the workers under new union contracts of 1,000 workers or more in the first half of 1971 but for only 27 percent in the first half of 1972 and 20 percent for all of 1972.[10] In manufacturing, first-year increases in union wage settlements averaged 8.3 percent in the first half of 1971, slightly above their 7.8 percent average rate for 1970, and declined substantially to 6.3 percent in the first half of 1972— although the corresponding decline for nonunion settlements was smaller, from 5.2 to 4.6 percent.[11]

---

[10] Bosworth, "Phase II: The U.S. Experiment with an Incomes Policy," Table 5, and *Annual Report of the Council of Economic Advisers*, 1973, p. 62.

[11] On wages and the Pay Board, see the essay by Marten Estey, this volume.

While controls had a substantial effect on union settlements, their overall impact on wages was less dramatic. Total compensation per man-hour for the private nonfarm sector rose 7.2 percent in the year ending June 1970 and 7.5 percent in the year ending June 1971; in the freeze and post-freeze catch-up periods combined (1971-III through 1972-I), it rose 6.2 percent at an annual rate, and then in the next two quarters decelerated to 5.2 percent. But in the fourth quarter of 1972 it shot up to an annual rate of 7.6 percent, and averaged 6.1 percent for the last three quarters of 1972. So the average deceleration was about 1½ percentage points. But this statistic is affected by cyclical changes in overtime pay. A better indicator is average hourly earnings for the private nonfarm sector adjusted for overtime in manufacturing and interindustry shifts, which exhibited a similar pattern but less deceleration. Its annual rate of increase was around 7 percent during 1970 and the first half of 1971. In the freeze and post-freeze catch-up (August 1971 through March 1972) it averaged 6.0 percent and, for the remainder of 1972, 6.3 percent. For this index the total deceleration from 1970 to the last three quarters of 1972 was less than 1 percentage point. Moreover, not all of this deceleration could be attributed solely to controls in view of the fact that a 6 percent unemployment rate persisted until June 1972 and a 5½ percent rate until November.

Unit labor costs decelerated considerably, as was noted, chiefly because of the stepped-up growth in output per man-hour beginning in early 1970. Thus prices could also decelerate and, at the same time, allow some improvement in depressed profit margins. To the extent that the reduction of inflation reflected a deceleration of unit labor costs, it was due primarily to business cost cutting and the economic recovery.[12]

If controls had a direct effect on prices in addition to the small indirect effect via wages, profit margins had to be squeezed. This indeed seems to be the explanation for the greater deceleration of prices under Phase II than during the year and a half preceding controls, a deceleration that was too sharp to be dismissed as accidental. Controls held back those price increases that would otherwise have occurred to improve profit margins. The margins generally advanced in 1971-72, to be sure, but presumably not as much as would otherwise have resulted from the business recovery. An effect of controls on profit margins is confirmed in an econometric

---

[12] Price controls had a temporary indirect effect on output per man-hour to the extent that they helped speed up the recovery in output.

study by Gordon.[13] He regressed the ratio of prices to unit labor costs on various explanatory variables and found that the predicted ratio was higher than the actual ratio under controls from the third quarter of 1971 to the second quarter of 1972. The implied reduction in the rate of inflation due to controls was 1¾ percent per year. The estimated effect on wages in his model was ¾ percent per year. While these results seem to underplay the effect of slack demand in curtailing inflation, they are consistent with the view that controls mainly affected profit margins.

The effect of price controls on profit margins works against market forces and distorts business incentives. Controls do not change the long-run relation between prices and unit labor costs determined by market forces. The margins will gravitate toward their market-determined levels, either through evasion of the controls or eventually when the controls are removed. There is then no lasting effect.

The deceleration in inflation initially produced by controls can have a lasting effect if it reduces the anticipated rate of inflation and the wage and price decisions that are influenced by anticipations. In a period of deceleration, anticipated price increases typically exceed the actual rate of inflation and thus help to keep the inflation going. Price controls that lead people to anticipate less inflation can make a net contribution to the efficiency and speed of the adjustment during the transition. On this view, the controls served as a policy announcement of the intended rate of inflation, possibly the only form of announcement that was believable, but with the added provision of forcing compliance to the extent that the policy was not believed.

The controls were minimally enforced upon all but the largest companies and unions, which was consistent with the view that anticipatory increases in prices and wages could be maintained only with "market power" and could be broken only by effectively restraining the use of such power. As was noted, however, large companies were not playing a critical role in the inflation. Most of the largest price increases were occurring in the least concentrated sectors, such as personal services, construction, food, and other basic commodities. Any lasting effect of controls, therefore, had to reduce the anticipated rate of inflation incorporated in union as well as nonunion wage increases. The impact on adjusted average hourly earnings was, as noted, about 1 percentage point—a third of the deceleration in the CPI from 6 to about 3 percent per year by the end of 1972. That is

---

[13] Robert J. Gordon, "Wage-Price Controls and Shifting Phillips Curve," *Brookings Papers on Economic Activity*, 2: 1972, Table 5.

indicative of the lasting effect of the controls via anticipations, and it is a maximum estimate because it includes the independent contribution of slack demand. The other two-thirds of the deceleration in consumer prices reflected improvements in productivity and a squeeze of profit margins due partly to slack demand and partly to the controls.

Other evidence on anticipations can be cited. The Dun and Bradstreet series on price changes expected by business purchasing agents pointed to modest reductions in anticipated inflation after August 1971, though the degree was not specified. Households surveyed by the University of Michigan Survey Research Center reported a decline in mean expected price changes from the second quarter of 1971 to mid-1972 of less than ¼ percentage point.[14] The decline in interest rates constituted a piece of indirect evidence, since these rates tend to incorporate the anticipated rate of inflation as compensation for depreciation in the purchasing power of borrowed funds. Short-term interest rates declined sharply following the imposition of controls in August 1971 but subsequently retraced most of their decline. They were influenced strongly by changing conditions in the money market, and their movements are difficult to interpret for this purpose. Long-term bond yields declined 26 basis points during the second half of August 1971 and further in subsequent months, for a total decline following the imposition of controls of about ½ percentage point. The CEA pointed to this as an indication of a decline in the anticipated rate of inflation.[15] Possibly demands for credit were working to raise interest rates in that period, and the effect of a reduction in the anticipated rate of inflation was greater than ½ percentage point. In any event, the reduction was much less than the deceleration in wage increases of 1 percentage point.

After the initial deceleration in wage increases from above 7 percent to 6 percent per year by the end of 1971, there was no further decline during 1972. With a trend growth in labor productivity of 3 percent per year, a wage increase of 6 percent was consistent with 3 percent inflation, to which any recovery in profit margins would be added. Notwithstanding the optimism with which the public first greeted the imposition of controls and the belief that inflation would somehow be eradicated quickly, it was winding down slowly. During most of 1972 slack in the economy created the conditions for a deceleration of inflation, and controls did not have to fight against

---

[14] George Katona, "A Communication: Inflation and the Consumer," *Brookings Papers on Economic Activity*, 3: 1972, pp. 788-790.

[15] *Annual Report of the Council of Economic Advisers*, 1973, p. 64.

the tide. This favorable situation lasted until nearly the end of the year and was deceptively conducive to an expansive monetary policy.

Monetary Policy and Business Activity under Controls. Notwithstanding the squeeze of profit margins, the Phase II controls did not produce the obvious restrictions on supplies that would be indicated by shortages and black markets. There is little evidence, therefore, that controls impeded the business recovery directly in the 1971-72 period.[16] They may have done so indirectly by creating uncertainty. The sluggish recovery of the first half of 1971 was no doubt prolonged to some extent into the third quarter by the uncertainties of international finance and of the price freeze. But the dark clouds soon cleared, and the expansion began to pick up by the fourth quarter. Then, in early 1972, as confidence grew that the economy would not be hamstrung by controls and that controls would somehow hold inflation in check, consumer expenditures rose and the laggard business recovery took off. Industrial production spurted. Real GNP rose 7.6 percent from the fourth quarter of 1971 to the fourth quarter of 1972. The increase in real GNP for the two years 1970-72 was stronger than in the two years following each of the cyclical recoveries beginning in 1954, 1958, and 1961, whereas comparison of real growth in just the first year of these recoveries shows 1971 to be the weakest. If a monthly indicator of real output (such as industrial production) is adjusted for the effect of the General Motors strike in the fourth quarter of 1970, the business contraction has the characteristics of a "flat bottom" with the end of the bottom occurring in August 1971. By this reckoning the recovery did not get off the ground until almost two years after the peak in November 1969.

Monetary policy had been highly conducive to a vigorous recovery in 1971. The money stock grew at a 6 percent rate during 1970 and 1971 following a 3 percent rate in 1969. Predicted increases in dollar GNP calculated according to the St. Louis monetary equation, based on actual money stock and high employment federal expenditures, are too high for the last three quarters of 1971 and way too high for the third quarter. The SSRC-MIT-PENN econometric model,

---

[16] There were special problems in lumber due to the profit ceilings. See "Lumber: Fumblings of the Visible Hand," First National City Bank, *Monthly Economic Letter*, December 1972. For other difficulties see "The Case Against Rigid Controls," by Assistant Secretary of the Treasury for Economic Policy Edgar R. Fiedler, in the *Wall Street Journal*, April 19, 1973, p. 20, and William Poole, "Wage-Price Controls: Where Do We Go From Here?" *Brookings Papers on Economic Activity*, 1: 1973.

in which the implicit lag in monetary effects is longer, also over-predicts but by less.[17] It is hard to know whether the international crisis and imposition of controls accounted for this delayed recovery despite the stimulative monetary growth, or whether other influences were at work.

In any event, the stubborn unemployment rate did not begin to decline until 1972, and then slowly at first because of increased growth in the labor force. This growth was finally absorbed, how-ever, and by year-end the unemployment rate fell to 5.1 percent. The decline in unemployment occurred despite continuing large gains in labor productivity. In the first three quarters of 1972 unit labor costs advanced at the lowest rates in many years, which made possible the slower price increases. All this had been programmed by policy makers to happen in 1971. But, for an administration facing an election in 1972, the long-sought improvement was most welcome.

Unfortunately, satisfaction with the cooling of inflation in the first half of 1972 led monetary policy to err on the expansive side, with disastrous results that did not become apparent until the year was over. The attitude that fostered this error was prophetically expressed at the beginning of the year in the 1972 *Annual Report of the Council of Economic Advisers:*

> The establishment of the direct wage-price controls created room for some more expansive measures, because it pro-vided a certain degree of protection against both the fact and the expectation of inflation. This situation had to be approached with caution, because excessive expansion could make the price-wage control system unworkable. Still there could be no doubt that the tolerable rate of expansion had been increased.[18]

The half-hearted plea for caution in this statement went unheeded.

---

[17] The predicted and actual values are as follows:

	Rate of Growth in GNP, 1971 (percent per year)		
	II	III	IV
Actual	7.9	5.4	8.3
St. Louis	9.8	12.4	9.1
SSRC-MIT-PENN	8.7	6.5	10.4

From E. Gerald Corrigan, "Income Stabilization and Short-run Variability in Money," Federal Reserve Bank of New York, *Monthly Review,* April 1973, pp. 87-98, Tables III and IV.

[18] *Annual Report of the Council of Economic Advisers,* 1972, p. 69.

In early 1972, anxious to speed the recovery of production, the Federal Reserve Open Market Committee called for "moderate" growth in the money stock, which apparently meant the same 6 percent average rate achieved during 1970 and 1971. But during the year the growth rate exceeded 6 percent in most months; it also experienced a sharp increase in July, which was not offset in subsequent months, and again in December due in part to the Treasury's year-end disbursement of revenue-sharing checks to state and local governments. The overall result for 1972 was monetary growth of 8.3 percent, and the increase for the year from January to January (which downplays the unintended December spurt) was still 8.2 percent.

The business recovery, which had proceeded sluggishly during 1971 and gathered speed slowly during the first part of 1972, now reached boom dimensions. Real GNP rose at an 8 percent annual rate in the final quarter of 1972 and first quarter of 1973. Production rose to near-capacity levels, triggering an expansion in business plans for investing in new capacity. Although wholesale prices of crude materials, foods in particular, had started rising rapidly in the latter part of 1972, they literally exploded in early 1973. Wholesale food prices rose at an annual rate of 47.5 percent seasonally adjusted in the first half of that year. Plausible-sounding explanations about special supply conditions were offered to minimize the inflationary significance of skyrocketing food prices. The chief explanation was the devaluation of the dollar, first in 1971 and again in January 1973, which had brought about higher domestic dollar prices for basic commodities traded on world markets. Also, the special sale of U.S. grains to Russia had reduced stocks, the beef-production cycle reached one of its periodic low points, and weather conditions were adverse for many farm products.

All these events contributed. Yet special conditions can always be found for certain products in a general inflationary upsurge. Rising aggregate demand was the major factor. While the first markets to reflect the business boom were as usual those for basic commodities, pressures on a broader range of prices came in due course. Wholesale prices of industrial commodities rose 12.5 percent at an annual rate seasonally adjusted in the first half of 1973 compared with 2.9 percent in the preceding half year. Even the less volatile prices of finished manufactured goods took off. The wholesale prices of consumer finished goods excluding foods experienced a rate of increase of 12.2 percent seasonally adjusted in the first half of 1973 compared with 2.1 percent in the preceding half year and

25

the rates for producer-finished goods were 5.2 percent in the later period and 1.2 percent in the earlier period (not adjusted). These price increases did not reflect temporary supply scarcities but the raging inflation of a business boom.

Incredibly, in the face of this new thrust of inflation, there was still no reduction in monetary growth by mid-1973. Even should it be reduced in the second half of the year, the usual lag in monetary effects of many months means that aggregate demand will remain strong for all of 1973 and well into 1974.

How can the failure of monetary policy to become even moderately restrictive after mid-1972 be explained? Understandably, the monetary authorities have not wished to thwart a business recovery, and it is difficult to achieve restraint in monetary growth when a business expansion is gaining strength. Reports of the Federal Reserve Open Market Committee indicated a desire early in 1972 for slower monetary growth than was being achieved. In February the committee began to state its monetary objectives in terms of reserves against private nonbank deposits, a statistical refinement which seemed to promise closer control over monetary growth. But rising short-term rates led to caution in pushing restraint too rapidly—though some members of the committee voted for a less expansionary policy. As was to be expected in a strong business recovery, short-term interest rates rose sharply. From a low of almost 3 percent in February 1972, Treasury bill yields rose to 4 percent by July, to 5½ percent in early 1973, and above 7 percent in May. Although long-term bond yields eased during the second half of 1972, they rose in 1973. The earlier appointment of Chairman Burns to head the Phase II committee charged with holding down increases in interest rates produced an unhelpful conflict of objectives here. Although the monetary growth rate declined somewhat during the second half of 1972 (except for the spurt in December), a majority of the Open Market Committee still harbored a traditional reluctance to abandon interest rates to the pull of market forces.

These reasons, however, could only partly account for the failure to achieve restraint for a whole year after mid-1972 by which time it had become clearly appropriate. Policy pursued a goal of driving the economy toward full employment without regard for the lag in monetary effects and for the need to slow the pace of economic expansion as the goal was approached. Given the well-recognized imprecision of forecasts and of monetary control over the economy, such a policy invited a resurgence of inflation. When it burst out, it was stronger than expected, but serious consequences should have been foreseen. During the painfully slow progress against inflation in 1969, 1970, and 1971, Federal Reserve and government authorities pledged not to fritter away the hard-won gains and repeat the mistake made in 1967 of overstimulating the economy as it recovered. But, in fact, the inflationary pressures which surfaced in early 1973 were much stronger than those which followed the monetary slowdown of 1966-67. They were hardly the temporary bubble of unfavorable supply conditions. The failure of policy in 1972 and early 1973 to restrain monetary growth was a monumental blunder.

Phase III as the Culprit. In January 1973 the administration relaxed the mandatory compliance of Phase II for all price and wage increases, except in food processing and distribution, construction wages, and health services, and substituted guidelines for the rest of the economy. The Price Commission and Pay Board were abolished, and the Cost of Living Council was authorized to see that the guidelines were followed. There was no intention of policing the guidelines, but mandatory controls could be reinstated on particular sectors if the guidelines were seriously breached. Pressure was to be applied primarily to the largest corporations and unions, but it was not used widely. Phase III guidelines were not rigid and offered more play to market forces. They started as a cross between the voluntary guideposts on wages and prices of the early 1960s, which had modest effects, and the mandatory but loosely enforced limits of Phase II.

The timing of the shift to Phase III led the public to believe that prices spurted because of the removal of Phase II controls. The amount of truth in this belief is miniscule. Although the ending of Phase II allowed firms to post catching-up price increases, most of the largest increases of early 1973 came in basic commodities which were uncontrolled under Phase II. Moreover, the pressures under prices that surfaced in 1973 had been building up for some months and would eventually have buckled the Phase II controls.

The administration ended Phase II in January 1973 under the impression that inflation was subsiding (showing once again that crucial economic turning points are seldom recognized at the time they occur) and that the economy seemed ready for uncontrolled prices, which the administration preferred. By chance, therefore, Phase II ended before its inability to contain a strong inflation was revealed. In a few months the public was clamoring for a tightening of price controls. The public outcry over soaring meat prices forced the administration to freeze them in March, and the broadening

27

inflationary pressures led to a second step back to controls in May, namely, the requirement that corporations with annual sales over $250 million gain prior approval of price increases above 1½ percent of the January 10 level.

During this period the administration resisted further increases in the federal budget and talked of applying monetary restraint to moderate the boom. These policies, together with larger agricultural supplies expected in the fall and continued moderation in wage increases, were thought to promise a desired cooling of inflation by the end of the year. It is true that some signs still pointed to that possibility. Output per man-hour for the private nonfarm sector rose 4.3 percent at an annual rate in the first quarter of 1973, up from 3.6 percent in the previous quarter, and this helped moderate the increase in unit labor costs. While the comparable rate for compensation per man-hour jumped from 7.6 percent in the preceding quarter to 10.4 percent (Table 1), much of this acceleration reflected increases in social security taxes and overtime pay. For negotiated wages and benefits in the first year of contracts covering 5,000 workers or more in all industries, decisions in the first quarter had an annual rate of increase of 7.3 percent, the same as in the preceding quarter and well below the rates of recent years. Wage increases for nonunion workers in manufacturing also continued to moderate. But, as the economy approached full capacity, substantial gains in productivity and continued moderation in wage demands became less likely. Although settlements during the first half of 1973 generally stayed within the guidelines, fears of union unrest figured prominently in the administration's willingness to tighten controls. As the resurgence of inflation broadened (with some increases no doubt occurring partly in anticipation of a change in Phase III rules), talk of the need and possibility of a new set of controls spread.

In June, Phase III ended with the imposition of a new freeze on all prices and wages except farm products (which were in effect controlled by the inability of processors and distributors to pass along any increases). This was followed in August by a Phase IV program similar to Phase II. The change in policy was intended to signal the failure of Phase III and its replacement with a "certified" program of controls. But Phase III mainly confirmed both the failure of monetary policy to moderate aggregate demand and the widespread appeal of rigid price controls despite the evidence of meager previous accomplishments. While the first freeze and Phase II did not disrupt the economy because demand was generally slack, the second freeze and Phase IV came when most markets were tight. For this reason, they are not able to avoid disruptions. There is also the danger that controls will further delay the pursuit of effective monetary restraint and so manage once again to produce just the opposite of their intended effect.

Choosing a Sustainable Monetary Policy against Inflation. The mistake of policy had been to push the economy toward full capacity at top speed with little chance of slowing the expansion before it burst into the zone of demand-pull inflation. This was simply reckless driving. Policy can safely nudge aggregate demand a little higher if the economy is growing at the desired speed along a path considered too low. But policy in 1973 faced the different and vastly more difficult task of slowing a rapid expansion and then holding it to the desired path after arriving there at an excessive speed. Long lags in monetary effects, which shorten the maneuvering time for achieving the appropriate growth rate of aggregate expenditures, can lead to such overshooting. The sharp braking of monetary restraint applied in response to overshooting can, further down the road, precipitate another recession.

With the economy again caught in a raging inflation, what should monetary policy do? Although the objective is clear—to put the economy on a growth path of stable prices and full employment— the position of the best path is uncertain and subject to dispute. Initially the administration had optimistically defined the optimum growth path as 4½ percent unemployment and 2½ percent inflation. But lately there has been a noticeable willingness to consider 3 to 3½ percent inflation as a commendable achievement (which acceptance of 6½ percent wage guidelines for 1973 also implies). Furthermore, doubts over the 4½ percent unemployment figure have grown. Continuing structural changes in the labor force, particularly the increased participation of women, suggest that normal turnover has made the noninflationary rate of aggregate unemployment higher than it formerly was.[19]

Although the desirable trend level of aggregate demand is in doubt, more confidence can be placed in the estimate of the rate of growth along the desired path. At full capacity the growth trend of output would be about 4½ percent per year—1¾ percent for growth in the labor force adjusted for a secular decline in hours of work and 2¾ percent for the long-run growth trend in output per

---

[19] See William Fellner's essay, this volume.

man-hour (assuming no growth for the government sector).[20] For a target rate of price increase of 2½ percent, the appropriate rate of increase in dollar GNP would be 7 percent per year, with smaller rates for any further declines in inflation. To translate the GNP target into an appropriate rate of monetary growth, we may look at the trend of money holdings. Since 1966 the ratio of dollar GNP to the money stock has been rising by 1½ percent per year, slower in the recession and faster in the recovery. For a boom year like 1973 with rising interest rates, the ratio might rise faster than trend for a while, but there is no basis for predicting a permanently higher rate. Given 7 percent growth in GNP, the corresponding growth for the money stock is 5½ percent.[21] A higher rate implies a faster growth in dollar GNP.

Compared with these estimated trends, the growth rates of 1972 and early 1973 of 7-8 percent were too high and had to be slowed. Moreover, expansions once under way have a self-propelling property which makes an overstimulative policy cumulatively too strong, particularly for sensitive markets like basic materials. Little can be done about the next several quarters without a drastic shift in policy. To avoid contributing to cycles of bust and then boom, the safest policy would seem to be to adhere to the desired long-run monetary growth rate of about 5 percent and let the inflationary resurgence due to the previous excessive growth take its course.

Summary and Evaluation

Progress against Inflation. When the present administration took office in 1969 and announced that curbing the inflation was its number one domestic priority, it thought the job would take two years at most. The 1955-59 inflation, which stood as a warning to this optimism, was generally forgotten. Yet, the present inflation has been even harder to subdue than previous ones, in part perhaps because it had lasted longer. First the excessive growth in aggregate demand had to be slowed by a cut in monetary expansion. The monetary restraint initially tightened financial markets and after a delay

---

[20] This is the figure for productivity growth usually cited. The growth since 1955, however, suggests that 2¾ percent is an overstatement. One projection for the 1970s is 2 percent per year (see William D. Nordhaus, "The Recent Productivity Slowdown," *Brookings Papers on Economic Activity*, 3: 1972, pp. 493-536). If correct, this lower figure means that the corresponding figures in the text should be reduced by ¾ percentage point.

[21] Or 4¾ percent using the 2 percent projection for productivity growth in the previous footnote.

slowed economic activity, which produced the 1970 recession. From the decision to restrain the economy to the beginning of the recession took a year by itself. Then, to general dismay, prices rose just as rapidly during the recession as they had before, carried along by the momentum of rising wages, costs, and anticipations of continuing inflation. The inflation rate reached a peak during 1970, but signs of a change in direction were unclear at the time, and no one could be sure that it had actually occurred. Many people concluded instead that the orthodox method of fighting inflation by restraining aggregate demand was a failure.

A process of unwinding the inflation was nevertheless at work beneath the surface. Excess productive capacity brought about by the business recession induced cost cutting. During the middle and later stages of the inflation, profit margins had fallen to low levels, and the recession-slack in demand and associated layoffs of workers created the conditions for intensified efforts to hold down costs. Output per man-hour, which had not advanced during 1969, began to improve markedly. Such improvement is typical of business contractions and recoveries, and in this instance it started in the second quarter of the recession, sooner than usual, and speeded up when business recovered. Many of the benefits of cost cutting completed earlier did not appear until later when production rose in the business recovery without the need for a commensurate addition to the work force. As productivity improved, unit labor costs decelerated appreciably despite the continuation of large wage increases. Initially this led to an improvement in profit margins rather than to smaller price increases. Historically, prices have reflected changes in unit costs after a lag of several quarters, and here too the growth of productivity exerted little restraint on price increases until the end of 1970, and then not as much at first as in past cycles.

By 1972, three years after the application of monetary restraint in 1969, the economy was finally recovering from the effects on output, and the inflation was half cured. The restraint had not been extraordinarily severe, and the execution of policy in 1969-70 was probably as competent as could reasonably be expected under practical circumstances. The problem had been the exasperating delay in getting results, a problem which indicates how long it takes to formulate and execute a change in direction for the economy. It is a sobering lesson for the future on the difficulties of recovering from an inflationary binge.

Price Controls. Phases I and II came in the midst of this process. Their effect is not easily determined because inflation was subsiding and would have continued to do so, at least for a while, even without controls and also because the strengthening business recovery during 1972 was bound to exert upward pressures on some prices that controls could not hold back. Adding to the difficulties of assessment, the key price indices differed in their measurement of the timing and extent of the initial deceleration. The CPI (excluding foods and mortgage interest) decelerated from a 6 percent annual rate of increase in 1970 to 4½ percent by mid-1971, *before* the imposition of controls, and to about 3 percent thereafter. The GNP deflator, on the other hand, decelerated from 5 to 2 percent per year, and the reduction came after mid-1971, *during* controls.

To be effective, controls have to hold down the advance of wage costs, and the Pay Board's success in chopping down some of the eye-catching union wage demands has been cited in support of Phase II. But the deceleration of wage increases in the economy at large was not great, and part of that reflected the slack in the economy. The increase in adjusted average hourly earnings fell from 7 percent in 1970 to 6 percent or so in 1972. It took time to slow the momentum of these increases, and, for some wages, the controls did well at first just to impede further acceleration.

Although much of the initial business support for controls presumed that they would curtail wage increases, their main contribution was to hold back the improvement in profit margins (controls had little to do with gains in output per man-hour). This effect could not be permanent, since the widely imagined profiteering[22]—an obvious target for controls—did not exist. Profit margins had declined sharply in 1969 and 1970 and remained low in 1971. They rose moderately with the business expansion in 1972 and finally spurted only with the surge of aggregate demand in the first quarter of 1973. Sooner or later profit margins gravitate to their market-determined levels. Controls can delay but not prevent those adjustments.

However, a temporary reduction in the inflation rate achieved by holding down profit margins might have lasting benefits if it contributed to lower anticipated rates of inflation. This, in turn, would reduce the upward pressure on wages and thence prices. Such a contribution is the main rationale for controls. But the maximum effect of Phase II on anticipations could not have exceeded the total deceleration of wages of one percentage point—and was much less

---

[22] In a Lou Harris poll of 1,537 households reported on May 14, 1973 in the *New York Post* (p. 6), 65 percent said that middlemen and processors were a "major cause" of the rise in food prices and an additional 21 percent said they were a "minor cause."

than that if household surveys and the small drop in long-term interest rates are the test. Apparently the anticipated rate of inflation was generally not much greater than the rate that the controls were expected to allow. Perhaps, too, anticipations of inflation played a much smaller role in price and wage setting compared with catching-up adjustments than this rationale for controls presumed.

Whatever limited effect controls had under the conditions of slack demand in 1971-72, a return to a freeze and rigid controls in the tight markets of 1973 makes no sense. Yet, despite the near-unanimity of professional economists that controls are not effective against demand-pull inflation, they have enormous appeal to the general public. The public believes that the relaxed Phase III controls were responsible for the surge of prices in 1973. Although the business community is now disillusioned with guidelines on prices, consumers want rigid controls and got them in June.

Monetary Policy. The price surge of 1973 did not result from the relaxation of Phase II controls, however. The business recovery, pushed along by stimulative monetary and fiscal policies during 1972, gradually gained strength and by year-end ran into demand-pull inflationary pressures. The devaluation of the dollar and special supply conditions contributed to large price increases in certain sectors, but the basic explanation was the brisk business expansion. Even had Phase II controls still been in effect during the first quarter of 1973, they could not have contained the spectacular increases in the prices of basic commodities, for these commodities were exempt under those controls.

Controls had the perverse effect of encouraging an overly expansive monetary policy. They led the authorities to believe that little of the monetary stimulation of aggregate demand would affect prices and nearly all of it would go to raise output. Monetary growth had averaged 6 percent per year in 1970 and 1971, which was reasonable for those years of slack demand. But it speeded up to 8 percent in 1972 and continued at 7 percent in the first half of 1973. To avoid overstimulation of the economy, policy should have slowly *reduced* monetary growth during 1972.

The failure to do so appears to be yet another case of the lag in monetary effects tripping up policy objectives. The previous case occurred during the mini-recession of 1967 when policy turned sharply expansive to stimulate economic recovery, only to find a year later that it had fueled another round of inflation. Policy makers vowed not to make that mistake again. The resurgence of inflation in 1973 shows that they have been no more successful this time. A flexible policy is supposed to avoid the cycle of bust to curb inflation followed by boom-producing expansions to speed the ensuing recovery. But a flexible policy is subject to the hazards and pressures of dealing with economic developments as they unfold. We are now back on square one in the battle against inflation, and the cumbersome reliance on government fiat to control prices only adds to the tragic consequences.

2

GRADUALISM AND THE NEW ECONOMIC POLICY

Fiscal Economics in Transition

Charles E. McLure, Jr.

The Nixon administration's early efforts to eliminate infla-tion through conventional techniques of demand manage-ment, without resort to incomes policy, failed, at least in the speed with which they brought results. Despite the economic softness that developed in 1970 and continued into 1971, fiscal stimulus was avoided in the name of fiscal responsi-bility. A presumptive rule of balance in the full-employ-ment budget should not prohibit discretionary fiscal policy when the economy is far from its target path. Finally, unless diligent efforts are made to maintain fiscal discipline, the nation faces the prospects of excess aggregate demand, rekindled inflation, and a subsequent recessionary adjust-ment. The confrontation between the Congress and the President over control of the budget shows dramatically the need for budgetary reforms that would provide fiscal discipline in the long run and flexibility in the short run.

Introduction and Conclusions

As 1973 began, public debate on fiscal policy centered upon how the full-employment budget could be kept in rough balance. The growing strength of the recovery from the 1970 recession suggested that well before the end of the year fiscal restraint would be needed. Yet, it did not appear likely that such restraint would materialize in the absence of a confrontation between the President and the Congress. In particular, in an environment in which the President did not want to divert a higher proportion of national output to (or through) the federal treasury and the Congress seemed to lack the will to raise taxes, even if it desired higher federal spending, the debate focused upon control of the federal budget. Simply put, at the end of 1972, the President had vetoed appropriation bills that he considered extravagant and had refused to spend appropriated funds in other cases. He claimed that these actions were necessary in the interest of fiscal responsibility, since the Congress seemed unable to hold total appropriations within the limits posed by full-employment revenues. Many observers viewed the President's actions as a usurpation of congressional prerogatives, and even more charitable observers feared a grave constitutional crisis.

The second major issue was whether or not the United States should continue, more or less permanently, the wage and price controls that were imposed as a freeze in August 1971, continued in a looser form by the Pay Board and Cost of Living Council under Phase II of the New Economic Policy (NEP), and finally relaxed still further in Phase III. Many economists believe that such controls can only work on the outward symptoms of inflation, and may do more harm than good. But many others, and especially many non-economists, probably feel that controls should be given much of the credit for whatever progress has been made in the fight against inflation and that some form of controls should be kept in the stabilization arsenal, if only on a standby basis.

In addition to the hotly debated questions of who controls—or should control—the public purse strings in the United States and of whether the United States should have a permanent incomes policy, several other questions have recently received considerable attention from economists. Perhaps the most basic of these is the choice of an unemployment rate to serve as the target of stabilization policy. Most economists agree that an unemployment rate of 4 percent—the "interim goal" set a decade ago by the Kennedy administration—is no longer consistent with price stability, if ever it once was, due to shifts in the composition of the labor force. One group of economists— whom for short we can call "non-accelerationists"—would argue that even if this were true, we need only choose a new optimal point on the shifted Phillips curve relating unemployment rates and (steady) rates of inflation, while continuing to improve the trade-off through structural policies. On the other hand, the "accelerationist" school denies that there exists a stable Phillips curve in the long run, arguing that if the unemployment rate is pushed below its natural level by aggregate demand, inflation will accelerate, rather than maintain a constant rate. Some members of this school go on to argue that if the global unemployment rate is to be reduced to anywhere near the

4 percent level without setting off an accelerating inflation, it will be necessary to take direct actions to reduce the unemployment rates among those groups who have historically experienced the highest rates of unemployment and who now comprise a larger share of the labor force than in the recent past.[1]

A second area of investigation that has been receiving increased attention from economists is how to make the economy self-stabilizing by instituting certain rules of fiscal "formula flexibility." This attention is predicated upon the historical evidence that policy makers cannot be trusted to take timely action to offset developing cyclical swings in the economy and that the existing built-in stabilizers are not likely by themselves to provide sufficient stability. Simply put, formula flexibility would provide that automatic variations in tax rates and expenditures would be induced by rises and falls in the level of economic activity.

These and other problems in the 1973 fiscal arena differed somewhat from the issues during most of the previous decade. Whereas professional opinion in early 1973 showed strong agreement that expansion was proceeding too rapidly and threatened to get out of hand, ten years ago economists were in general agreement that an overly restrictive fiscal policy was preventing the attainment of full employment and was stifling economic growth. But they disagreed upon whether fiscal policy should be active or passive once full employment was attained. When taxes were cut in 1964, the economy responded strongly, as expected. But before it became necessary to define the full-employment level of output more precisely than in terms of an interim goal of a 4 percent unemployment rate and before we had time to gather evidence on whether fiscal policy at full employment—however defined—should be active or passive, we were faced with another issue. Just as the 4 percent unemployment rate was reached, spending on the Vietnam War and the Great Society increased and the foremost fiscal question became whether the United States would have the will to raise taxes or forgo some federal spending. When that question was answered in the negative, inflation began. And when the Federal Reserve attempted to buck the tide of federal red ink in 1966 by hauling in on the monetary reins, another question in the sphere of stabilization policy was answered. Money,

---

[1] A hybrid view holds that a stable Phillips curve exists for fairly high levels of the unemployment rate (and low inflation rates), but that once the unemployment rate nears 4 percent, inflation will begin to accelerate. This theory is presented in Otto Eckstein and Roger Brinner, *The Inflation Process in the United States* (Washington, D. C.: Joint Economic Committee, 1972), along with references to other literature on the subject.

as well as fiscal policy, matters—but it matters especially for housing and state and local governments. When taxes were finally raised in the middle of 1968, we got an answer for a question that few had bothered to ask. Temporary changes in income tax rates seem to have had relatively less impact on personal and corporate spending than had been expected.

The Nixon administration's tenure in the White House began with a pronouncement of faith in the ability of aggregate stabilization policies gradually to reduce the rate of inflation to acceptable levels without causing an unacceptable rise in the unemployment rate and a disavowal of the use of any kind of incomes policy. The experience of two-and-one-half years of "gradualism" cast considerable doubt upon the wisdom of fighting inflation through monetary and fiscal policy alone and, in August 1971, the Nixon administration imposed a ninety-day freeze on prices and wages. During 1972, significant progress was finally made against both inflation and unemployment. More progress was expected in 1973, but an unfortunate combination of supply-related pressures on prices (especially for food and fuel) and the threat posed by an overly rapid expansion now cloud the picture.

As the unemployment rate falls below 5 percent, the "terms of trade" between unemployment and inflation, if indeed there are any, will come under increasing scrutiny, as will the question of whether fiscal policy should be active or passive. But foremost in everyone's mind for the immediate future will be the resolution of the power struggle between the President and the Congress for control of federal spending. Even so, it seems worthwhile to glance back at the experience of the last four years to see what lessons for the future can be learned from the conduct of fiscal policy during that period. The purpose of this essay is to provide such a backward glance. The first section reviews briefly the highlights of the economic doctrines, policies, and performance of the Kennedy-Johnson years in order to provide a historical backdrop for what follows. Since a previous essay in this series covers these years in detail, the review here is brief indeed and can be passed over by readers familiar with the economic history of the period.[2] The second section reviews in some-

---

[2] Charles E. McLure, Jr., *Fiscal Failure: The Lessons of the Sixties* (Washington: American Enterprise Institute, 1972), also published as a chapter in Phillip Cagan, Marten Estey, William Fellner, Charles E. McLure, Jr., and Thomas Gale Moore, *Economic Policy and Inflation in the Sixties* (Washington: American Enterprise Institute, 1972), pp. 7-87. References are kept to a minimum in the first and second sections since the subjects discussed there are covered in greater detail in this earlier essay. Throughout this essay, all references to budgetary magnitudes are to the government sector of the national income accounts (NIA) unless the contrary is stated explicitly.

what greater detail the stabilization policies followed by the Nixon administration before August 1971, though this period is also covered by the earlier essay. Experience since the freeze is discussed in substantially greater detail next and the final section offers an assessment of fiscal policy since 1969. The remainder of this introduction summarizes the most important conclusions of the essay.

First, there can be little doubt that the initial Nixon efforts to disinflate and restimulate the economy during the period before August 1971 were a failure, if only in the speed with which they bore fruit. Although the unemployment rate rose to the neighborhood of 6 percent, the rate of inflation showed little inclination to fall quickly to acceptable levels in response to intentionally engineered softness in the economy. Second, it is unfortunate that Nixon did not adopt some variant of an incomes policy earlier, once excess aggregate demand had subsided. Attempting to squeeze inflation out of the economy through demand management policies alone aggravated both the depth and length of the recession and the slowness of the recovery that followed. And because of the impact upon expectations, it is doubly unfortunate that Nixon announced shortly after coming to the White House that he would not interfere in private wage and price decisions.

Third, over much of the Nixon period before August 1971 fiscal policy was too restrictive. This is in part the natural consequence of the decision to fight inflation solely through demand management, without an assist from any kind of incomes policy. But it also reflects the development of a new fiscal orthodoxy which demands that, except in emergencies, expenditures (unified budget) should not exceed the revenues that the tax system would yield if the economy were operating at full employment. As a general presumptive rule, budget balance at full employment makes sense and is vastly superior to the old orthodoxy that required balance in the actual budget. Had it been adhered to, such a presumptive budgetary rule would have prevented much of the inflation that began in 1966. And of more immediate relevance, it would contribute to the maintenance of fiscal responsibility in 1973 and beyond. But it does not seem wise to prohibit ourselves from using discretionary fiscal policy in a situation such as prevailed during late 1970 and early 1971.

Our fourth conclusion is, then, that we should adopt a presumption that the unified budget should be in rough balance at full employment, but that we should stand ready to use discretionary and temporary tax changes when necessary to keep the economy close to the target path. As has been proposed so many times in the past, these could be across the board (positive or negative) surcharges on the income taxes, imposed at the President's discretion but subject to congressional approval. Going a step further, consideration could be given to a variable tax subsidy for business fixed investment and expenditures on consumer durables or to formula flexibility, under which tax rates would vary automatically with economic conditions. In any event, decisions about the level of taxation that is appropriate for short-run stabilization purposes should be divorced from decisions about the optimal level of taxes and expenditures in the long run, this latter being based on the desirability of various government programs.

Finally, institutional innovations are necessary to improve decisions on the proper level of taxes and government expenditures and to ensure that in normal (full employment) times taxes cover expenditures. The twin specters of congressional unwillingness to raise the taxes needed to pay for programs authorized and presidential usurpation of the financial prerogatives of the Congress are both unacceptable and fraught with danger.

Kennedy-Johnson Economics

When John Kennedy became President in 1961, the U.S. economy was operating at well below its potential and had been doing so for three years. Reflecting the relatively depressed level of output, the unemployment rate for those three years had averaged almost 6 percent and it rose during 1961 to average 6.7 percent for the year as a whole. On the brighter side, prices were relatively stable over this period, again reflecting the low level of economic activity and the absence of demand-pull pressures.

The New Economics. The economists advising President Kennedy argued—and most other economists agreed—that the economy's failure to operate at capacity could be traced directly to an overly restrictive fiscal policy. During 1960 and 1961, for example, the federal sector of the national income and product account would have shown an average surplus of $11 billion, or 2.2 percent of potential GNP, if the economy had operated at full employment. That the budget (NIA basis) was approximately in balance for the two years reflected the shortfall in revenues produced by the failure of potential output to be achieved, not a "neutral" fiscal policy.

Because this high full-employment surplus constituted unhealthy fiscal restraint, the argument went, taxes should be cut—as they were in 1964—in order to reduce the full-employment surplus and allow the economy to reach full employment, which at that time was taken tentatively to be 4 percent. Monetary policy would be largely "accommodative," by allowing the expansion to proceed without being choked off by high interest rates.

As unemployment was reduced, it would be necessary to know the shape of the Phillips curve, which showed the trade-off between inflation and unemployment, in order to determine whether the unemployment rate could be pushed below the 4 percent interim target without generating inflationary pressures. As the unemployment rate was reduced, inflationary pressures would grow. But these pressures should not be great if full employment were approached gradually, especially in the final stages of the approach. Moreover, it was believed that wage-price guideposts and presidential jawboning could contribute significantly to the prevention of inflation stemming from above-average price and wage increases in concentrated portions of the economy. Once full employment was reached, the economy would be kept on or near the growth path of potential output by the timely application of the fiscal stimulus or restraint indicated to be necessary by econometric forecasts of economic conditions.

There were, of course, dissenting views from the glowing picture of an economic Camelot painted by the Kennedy Council of Economic Advisers. The most important of these was the one associated most commonly with Milton Friedman and with the Committee for Economic Development (CED) and its research director, Herbert Stein. Though the Friedman and CED views were not identical, they shared the belief that discretionary fiscal policy is as likely to be destabilizing as stabilizing, and that it is likely to have a natural bias toward full-employment deficits and inflation. From this belief it was concluded that tax rates and expenditure policies should be set so as to yield rough balance or a small surplus at full employment and not varied for countercyclical reasons. Fiscal policy would contribute to the maintenance of economic stability only through the built-in stabilizers in the budget, inherent especially in the responsiveness of tax revenues (at unchanged rates) to changes in economic activity. Of course, advocates of the so-called stabilizing budget agreed with their more activist colleagues that a reduction in the full-employment surplus was needed in the early 1960s, even though they disagreed as to the course policy should follow once full employment was neared.

Origins of Inflation. Taxes were cut in 1964 and the economy behaved much as had been predicted by the so-called new economics. By the

41

end of 1965, the unemployment rate stood at 4.0 percent. Equally important, this impressive result had been achieved with little cost in terms of a higher rate of inflation. Though the economic advance in late 1965 was somewhat more rapid than expected or desired, it seemed reasonable to believe that slight pressure would be applied to the fiscal brakes in order to allow the economy to slide smoothly onto the long-run path of potential output without creating serious inflationary pressures.

This belief was short-lived. Although expenditures for the Vietnam War and domestic Great Society programs were rising rapidly, President Johnson refused to request in early 1966 the tax increase his economic advisers warned was necessary if inflation was to be avoided. In addition, and perhaps as a direct result of this fiscal inaction, businessmen added fuel to the developing inflationary fires by investing heavily in plant and equipment, sensing that demand would be strong for the foreseeable future. Through most of 1966 only the Federal Reserve resisted strongly the trend toward inflationary excess aggregate demand, holding down the growth in the money supply in the face of increasing demands for credit. This abandonment of an accommodative monetary policy sent interest rates soaring and residential construction plummeting. Even so, the unemployment rate fell below the interim 4 percent goal, to 3.8 percent, for the year as a whole. More important, the consumer price index (CPI) and the implicit GNP deflator both rose by over 3 percent during 1966. Finally, by the end of 1966 wage-price guideposts and jawboning had lost whatever effectiveness they had had in the war against inflation, though the Council of Economic Advisers continued to announce guideposts throughout the remainder of the Johnson administration and even in its 1969 annual report.

The end of the investment boom, which may simply have run its course or may have been stifled by the temporary suspension of the investment tax credit in late 1966, together with a sizable inventory adjustment and continued weakness in homebuilding, produced a slight downturn of economic activity in early 1967, despite the continuation of a strongly expansionary fiscal policy. Nevertheless, it was predicted that recovery in the second half of the year would be strong, and in his 1968 budget message, President Johnson requested a 6 percent income tax surcharge, to be effective July 1, 1967. Administration economists hoped that finally they could put the economy on its long-range growth path of full employment with price stability, despite the difficulties of doing so in the presence of the increasing commitment to the Vietnam War and domestic social programs.

Once again the economists' hopes were thwarted by political realities. Partly because of reluctance to raise taxes before it saw hard evidence that higher taxes were needed and partly because of disagreement with Johnson as to the importance of higher expenditures for the Vietnam War and domestic programs, the Congress delayed passage of the surcharge—which it finally enacted at a 10 percent rate—until mid-1968. Because of this delay, the full-employment deficit rose to average over $11 billion (at an annual rate) during the four quarters immediately preceding imposition of the surcharge. Such a strongly stimulative fiscal policy coming at a time of high employment and renewed strength in private demand was to have woefully predictable results.

What seems not to have been fully anticipated, however, even by most professional economists, was the relatively small impact the surcharge would have on private spending in the short run. Households appear to have reacted to the surcharge by saving less, as much as by consuming less, and corporations continued to invest at a high rate in spite of the surcharge. Moreover, the Federal Reserve, fearing that the disinflationary medicine would be too much for its overheated patient, reacted to the surcharge by expanding the money supply at what turned out to be a much too rapid rate. Because of the delay in passing the surcharge and because of the surcharge's weakness and the perversity of the monetary policy accompanying it, unemployment during 1968 averaged only 3.6 percent of the labor force and inflation accelerated. (From December 1967 to December 1968, the CPI and the wholesale price index (WPI) rose by 4.7 percent and 2.8 percent, respectively.) But perhaps more important in retrospect, though more difficult to measure even now, Americans seemed increasingly to have come to view inflation as an ordinary, if not pleasant, part of life during the late 1960s.

In summary, the 1964 tax cut produced the welcome advance to high employment that had been predicted, and apparently with little pressure on prices. But the failure to raise taxes to finance increased spending on the Vietnam War and domestic programs allowed the full-employment budget to shift far into the red and drove the economy well beyond the mere achievement of full employment. As a result, excess aggregate demand caused inflation to begin and then to accelerate, and the guideposts crumbled. By the time the surcharge was passed in 1968, inflation was proceeding at a rapid rate and strong inflationary expectations had been generated. Finally, the surcharge had substantially less impact on spending than might have been expected, perhaps in a large part due to the shift to a highly expansionary monetary policy that accompanied its passage.

Lessons of the Sixties. The inflationary experience of the late 1960s provided us with some important new information about the economy in some areas, but left us with a substantial amount of uncertainty in others. One critical piece of economic information that the inflationary fiasco of the late 1960s prevented us from obtaining was direct evidence on the trade-off between price stability and high employment. It seems possible that in the mid-1960s a 4 percent unemployment rate could have been maintained indefinitely without serious pressure on prices, especially if it had been approached gradually and if active measures were taken to improve the unemployment-inflation trade-off. And it is even possible—if less likely— that the unemployment rate could have been safely pushed somewhat below 4 percent, provided it were reduced very slowly and carefully. Certainly it could not be pushed down quickly, as it was in 1966 and 1968, without disastrous effects on the rate of inflation.

The experience of the late 1960s should have settled rather conclusively one of the more curious debates in modern economics. The 1966 credit crunch, which slowed the growth of aggregate demand in the face of a highly expansionary fiscal policy and which was repeated in a somewhat different form and intensity in 1969, showed convincingly that "money matters." But this and the later experience revealed that, due in large part to institutional rigidities, money matters most to residential construction and state and local government financing, an allocative result that some observers have concluded renders extremely tight money an unacceptable means of controlling aggregate demand.[3]

While the experience of the late 1960s showed conclusively that money matters, though unevenly, it did not similarly provide a conclusive test of the efficacy of an active fiscal policy of the type espoused by the Kennedy-Johnson economists. The nation was not allowed to gain experience under an activist fiscal policy operating in an environment of full employment achieved gradually and without inflationary pressures. Just as full employment was being

---

[3] See, for example, the discussion by Arthur M. Okun, "Rules and Roles for Fiscal and Monetary Policy," in James J. Diamond, ed., *Issues in Fiscal and Monetary Policy: The Eclectic Economist Views the Controversy* (Chicago: De Paul University, 1971), pp. 51-74, esp. pp. 54-55. The institutional rigidities include maximum interest rates that can be paid on state and local debt and charged on FHA mortgages.

achieved, fiscal policy assumed a stance that President Johnson's advisers knew was inappropriately expansionary and invalidated the test. The advocate of activism in fiscal policy might plead that both the inflation and the failure of the 1968 surcharge to have the anticipated effect should be traced to the politicians who allowed excess demand to build up and not to the new economics, since the latter, if followed consistently, would have prevented the inflationary binge and made the surcharge unnecessary.

In response to this line of thought, the advocate of the stabilizing budget approach to fiscal policy might note that his advocacy was based in part precisely upon the danger that when it mattered most, political forces would prevent required fiscal steps from being taken. According to this view, the inflation of the 1960s, far from invalidating the test of the new economics, should be interpreted as a low score on the test.

On the basis of evidence from the late 1960s, advocates of the CED rule seem to have been correct.[4] Certainly the CED rule that the full-employment budget should show a slight surplus at full employment, had it been followed, would have prevented the massively inflationary deficits at (more than) full employment that occurred. But as even the architects of the CED rule (especially Herbert Stein) have argued, it is not obvious who could have imposed such a rule upon the Congress and the President, or how. Quite possibly the same influences that prevented the appropriate fiscal actions from being taken between late 1965 and mid-1968 in the absence of a rule requiring that the full-employment budget be in approximate balance would have caused the rule to be broken, if it had existed.

In short, those who entered the 1960s with high hopes for the stabilizing possibilities of an active fiscal policy had those hopes treated rather badly, first by fiscal inaction originating in the political sphere, and then by the weakness of the impact of the 1968 income tax surcharge on aggregate demand. The experience must have caused almost all advocates of the new economics to temper with caution their enthusiasm for the possibilities of "fine tuning." And

---

[4] In personal conversation with the author, Frank W. Schiff, chief economist for the CED, has taken exception to the repeated references to the CED rule in McLure, *Fiscal Failure: The Lessons of the Sixties*, because the CED in its policy statement, *Fiscal and Monetary Policies for Steady Economic Growth* (New York, 1969), had recognized that stabilization objectives may call for discretionary fiscal actions to supplement the built-in stabilizers in the budget. Reference in the earlier essay was, of course, to the CED rule as it had existed throughout most of the 1960s and as it was commonly understood by the public. The importance of modifications to the original rule and their relation to the policies of the current administration are discussed below.

it demonstrated quite clearly the dangers of ever letting the economy become overheated by pursuing an overly expansionary fiscal policy. Experience under the surcharge suggested that the success of "fine tuning" was likely to be greater if the "coarse tuning" knob had not first been twisted violently.

The Game Plan of Gradualism

By the time Richard Nixon became President in 1969, the nation had returned from the fiscal insanity of the 1966-68 period. The tax surcharge and expenditure controls passed in 1968 had reduced the full-employment deficit from almost $11 billion (at an annual rate) in the first half of that year to just over $4 billion in the second half, and for 1969 as a whole the full-employment budget showed a surplus of $11.7 billion.[5] Partly offsetting this tight fiscal policy, which resulted in part from the continuation of the 10 percent surcharge until the end of 1969, was a marked loosening of monetary policy by the Federal Reserve in late 1968. Due to the fear of fiscal overkill, the money supply was allowed to grow almost twice as fast during the second half of the year as during the first.

President Nixon's economic advisers believed that by continuing this restrictive fiscal policy—which would now be combined with tight money—they could eliminate the excess aggregate demand that had spawned the inflation, and do so without inducing any important rise in the unemployment rate. After a short period of relatively harmless disinflation during which inflationary expectations would be broken, prices would be rising substantially more slowly than before and the economy could be restimulated to put it on the path of full employment and price stability. The quest for a fiscal Camelot, at least, had become a bipartisan objective.

As first steps in implementing this policy, the Nixon administration announced its support for the extension of the surcharge through the middle of 1970, its intention to hold federal spending in fiscal

---

[5] The 1968 figures are from Arthur M. Okun and Nancy H. Teeters, "The Full Employment Surplus Revisited," *Brookings Papers in Economic Activity*, 1: 1970 (Washington, D. C.: The Brookings Institution, 1970), pp. 104-106, and the 1969 figures are from the *Annual Report of the Council of Economic Advisers*, 1971 (Washington, D. C.: U.S. Government Printing Office, 1971), p. 73. The figures are not quite consistent, in that the CEA estimate of the full-employment deficit for 1968 as a whole is $6.0 billion, whereas the Okun and Teeters estimate is $7.6 billion. Similarly, the 1969 estimate by Okun and Teeters is only $9.8 billion. But the two sets of figures tell the same story in general terms.

1970 some $2.4 billion below the amount requested in the final Johnson budget, and its desire to see the 7 percent investment tax credit removed from the books, this last to be a permanent change. For its part, the Federal Reserve strongly reversed directions and, during 1969, the money supply grew by barely 3 percent.

Initially this policy of gradualism was generally accepted as being reasonable in broad form (if not in terminology) by most economists. Where President Nixon's advisers and their Democratic counterparts differed were (1) on the conduct of policy after reasonable price stability and full employment were attained and (2) on the usefulness of wage and price guideposts or controls.

Not surprisingly, the Nixon Council of Economic Advisers, in which Herbert Stein assumed primary responsibility for fiscal policy, early announced a goal for budgetary policy that resembled closely the CED rule.[6] It explicitly eschewed the activist fiscal stance embraced by its predecessors under the unfortunate name of "fine tuning," though in fact the tightrope it hoped to walk in the return to full employment and price stability was exceedingly thin.

Moreover (and ironically when seen in retrospect), the Nixon administration almost immediately upon assuming office announced that it would use neither wage-price guideposts or controls nor presidential jawboning in its efforts to halt inflation. This disavowal of any form of incomes policy, which was gratuitously repeated many times and roundly criticized by Democrats, was based upon several fundamental beliefs. These were (1) that an incomes policy could have no real and lasting effect on the rate of inflation so long as inflation was due to excess aggregate demand; (2) that such a policy would be unnecessary once aggregate demand was reduced to a level consistent with full employment and price stability, as softness in labor and product markets would automatically and fairly quickly reduce the rates of price and wage increases to acceptable levels; and (3) that by interfering with the free market allocation of resources an incomes policy maintained for any length of time would be positively harmful.

The Gradual Effects of Gradualism. The combination of tight monetary and fiscal policies pursued during 1969 did have the desired effect of slowing the growth of GNP, though the effect was slow in coming and was felt more in terms of slower real growth than in terms of lower rate of inflation. In real terms, GNP grew by only

---

[6] See *Annual Report of the Council of Economic Advisers*, 1970, pp. 67-68.

2.7 percent in 1969, well below the long run potential rate, estimated at 4¼ percent, and in the fourth quarter real output was actually slightly below its third quarter level. Even so, the unemployment rate was 3.5 percent in December. Moreover, the rate of inflation showed no inclination to fall, and in fact the rate of price increase accelerated somewhat over its 1968 level. Finally, the effects of monetary restraint were felt primarily in the markets for state and local securities and capital projects and in mortgage lending and residential construction.

Nixon's Council of Economic Advisers proposed in its 1970 annual report to continue the policy of gradualism it had followed during 1969. Under this policy softness would be allowed to develop early in the year, in order to reduce inflationary pressures and inflationary expectations. Then recovery in the second half would prevent unemployment from rising to unacceptable levels. For the year as a whole an unemployment rate of no more than 4.3 percent and a rate of inflation of about 4.4 percent, as measured by the GNP deflator, were expected.

In operational terms, this meant that a modest surplus in the unified budget would be combined with "moderate monetary restraint" in 1970. This combination, it was claimed, would allow both achievement of the target path of GNP and the recovery of residential construction and state and local borrowing, which had been especially hard hit by the monetary restraint of 1969. Strangely enough, the 1970 annual report of the CEA, written in large part under the direction of Herbert Stein, one of the early architects of the concept, contains no estimate of the balance in the full-employment budget. But Okun and Teeters estimated that the full-employment budget would show a surplus of $10 billion for the year as a whole.[7] This did not appear too restrictive at the time, as most economists agreed that any slowdown would be mild.

The economy's performance was even more disappointing in 1970 than it had been in 1969. The GNP deflator rose just as rapidly—by 5.3 percent—as in the previous year. And the unemployment rate rose to an average of 4.9 percent for the entire year, and stood at 6.2 percent at the end of the year. In real terms, GNP was

---

[7] Okun and Teeters, "The Full Employment Surplus Revisited." In response to questions posed in the Joint Economic Committee's hearings on its *Annual Report*, the CEA did offer both some alternative estimates of the full-employment surplus and a discussion of why such estimates were a particularly unsatisfactory measure of the state of the budget at that time. Some of these points also appear in Okun and Teeters, ibid.

below its third-quarter 1969 level in each quarter of 1970. Though the figures for output were made worse by the General Motors strike in the fourth quarter, there could be no doubt that the Nixon policy of gradualism was affecting real output and the unemployment rate much more strongly than it was affecting the rate of inflation—and also much more strongly than had been expected. Even so, the situation on the output and employment side, if not on the inflation side, would probably have been even worse if the full-employment surplus had not fallen by $3.5 billion in the course of the year, to $6.7 billion, because of the administration's inability to hold spending within the limits it had set for itself. In retrospect, even this full-employment surplus seems to have been too large and the administration's dogged commitment to budgetary restraint ill-advised, given the continued weakness of the economy. Moreover, the 5½ percent increase in the money supply might have been somewhat below the rate that would have been appropriate, given the continuing rate of inflation.

In its 1971 annual report the Council of Economic Advisers repeated its determination to follow the initial game plan of gradualism, though the American public must have felt by then that the administration was playing in economic overtime. In a forecast that was as much a target as a prediction and that many outside observers believed must have been mandated by the White House, the CEA predicted that GNP for 1971 would total $1,065 billion. This, it announced, would be "consistent with satisfactory progress towards . . . an unemployment rate in the 4½ percent zone and an inflation rate approaching the 3 percent range by mid 1972." [8] Not surprisingly, this extremely optimistic GNP forecast, and with it the corollary effects in terms of inflation and unemployment, met with general disbelief on the part of forecasters whose GNP figures were bunched fairly tightly in the range of $1,045 to $1,050 billion. Much of the skepticism arose because it did not appear that policy would be stimulative enough to produce a recovery of this strength from such a mild recession. [9]

The Keynesianism of Nixon. Probably more important in the long run than this unrealistically high forecast was the official endorsement by President Nixon of the concept of the full-employment budget. Citing both the need to avoid balancing the actual budget

---

[8] *Annual Report of the Council of Economic Advisers,* 1971, p. 84.

[9] This forecast was generally received more favorably by outside economists leaning toward the monetarist school than by those with fiscalist tendencies.

when the economy is operating at below its potential and the need for fiscal discipline, the President said:

> In fiscal 1971, the Federal Government will spend $212.8 billion, which is equivalent to the revenues the economy would be generating at full capacity. The actual deficit is expected to be $18½ billion. In fiscal 1972, also, the planned expenditures are equivalent to the revenues we would get at full employment. How big the actual deficit will be next year, in fiscal 1972, will depend on economic conditions. If the economy follows the expected path of a vigorous, noninflationary expansion, the deficit will decline to $11½ billion. This combination of deficits is appropriate to the situation through which the economy has been passing. The budget moved into deficit during calendar 1970 as the economy lagged below its potential. Accepting this deficit helped to keep the decline in the economy moderate. It was a policy of not subjecting individuals and businesses to higher tax rates, and of not cutting back Federal spending, when the economy is weak because such actions would have weakened economic conditions further.
>
> To say that deficits are appropriate in certain conditions is not to say that deficits are always appropriate or that the size of the deficit is ever a matter of indifference. Such a policy of free-for-all deficit financing would be an invitation to inflation and to wasteful spending.
>
> As I stated last June, we need to abide by a principle of budget policy which permits flexibility in the budget and yet limits the inevitable tendency to wasteful and inflationary action. The useful and realistic principle of the full employment budget is that, except in emergencies, *expenditures should not exceed the revenues that the tax system would yield when the economy is operating at full employment*. The budget for fiscal 1972 follows this principle.
>
> Balancing the budget at full employment does not deny or conceal the deficit that will exist this year and almost certainly next year. It does, however, avoid large deficits when they would be inflationary, like the swing to a big deficit in fiscal 1968. It means that even when the economy is low we must not allow our expenditures to outrun the revenue-producing capacity of the tax system, piling up the prospect of dangerous deficits in the future when the economy is operating at a high level. Moreover, to say that expenditures must not exceed the full employment revenues draws a clear line beyond which we must not raise the budget unless we are willing to pay more taxes. This is an

irreplaceable test of the justification for spending. It keeps fiscal discipline at the center of budget decisions.[10]

These pronouncements were interpreted—and probably rightly so—as heralding the acceptance by Richard Nixon of a sizable portion of the gospel of Keynesian economics, though we should hasten to add, "the gospel according to George Shultz, Paul McCracken, and Herbert Stein." In particular, they implied that no effort would be made to offset tendencies toward budgetary deficits induced by softness in the economy. But the Nixon conversion to Keynesian economics did not extend to the discretionary use of fiscal policy in the form of a full-employment deficit to stimulate recovery. Devotion to maintaining balance in the full-employment budget precluded that. Thus in the short run the administration pegged its hopes for a rapid recovery—and achievement of its $1,065 billion target for GNP—upon monetary policy, the built-in stabilizers in the budget, and the tendency of the economy towards full employment.[11]

Finally, in its 1971 annual report the CEA again repeated its disavowal of the kind of direct controls on wages and prices that would be instituted less than seven months later. After noting public weariness with continued inflation and support for direct wage and price controls, the council catalogued some of the hidden dangers in such controls and made the following statement: "Short of an emergency of a kind which does not exist, mandatory comprehensive price and wage controls are undesirable, unnecessary, and probably unworkable. The Government should not rely upon pseudo-solutions for real problems and should not delude the public about doing so." [12] It did, however, note the role played by inflationary expectations and the desire to "make up" for past losses due to unanticipated inflation in giving "momentum" to the existing inflation and in prolonging inflation. Thus, while the CEA continued to express its belief in the efficacy of conventional stabilization measures, it was beginning to admit more explicitly that something more drastic might need to be done if ever inflationary expectations were to be broken.[13]

---

[10] *Economic Report of the President,* 1971 (Washington, D. C.: U.S. Government Printing Office, 1971), pp. 6-7. Actually, Nixon had officially sanctioned use of the full-employment budget concept during July of 1970, though an occasional statement by him and various high administration officials after that seemed to belie the fact.

[11] The administration announced the liberalization of depreciation rules at the start of 1971. But this was not expected to provide much stimulus during 1971; see *Annual Report of the Council of Economic Advisers,* 1972, p. 33.

[12] *Annual Report of the Council of Economic Advisers,* 1971, pp. 78-82. The quotation is from p. 80.

[13] See *Annual Report of the Council of Economic Advisers,* 1971, pp. 60-62 for the CEA's discussion of "Why Is the Inflation So Stubborn?"

CHARLES E. MCLURE, JR.

Nixon's New Economic Policy

Gradualism seems to have been slightly more successful during the first seven-and-a-half months of 1971 than it had been during the previous two years—but only slightly. Real output rose by 8 percent (annual rate) in the first quarter, due partly to the recovery from the effects of the General Motors strike, but the rate of increase fell to 3.4 percent in the second quarter. For the year ending with the third quarter of 1971, GNP rose by 7.1 percent, the rise being split between a 4.6 percent increase in the GNP deflator and a 2.4 percent increase in the real output. This growth in real output was insufficient to produce any substantial fall in the unemployment rate, which varied narrowly about the 5.9 to 6.0 percent range for the first seven months and stood at 6.1 percent in August.

The increase in GNP during this year was fueled by extraordinarily large increases in residential construction and purchases of state and local governments, two components of demand that had been hit hard by tight money in the earlier periods and were rebounding in response to easier credit conditions. (Partly because early figures understated the growth in the money supply during the first quarter and partly because the Federal Reserve gauged the rate of monetary expansion by looking at money market conditions, the money supply grew at an annual rate of 10 percent during the first half of the year.) Business-fixed investment and federal purchases added little to aggregate demand, and inventory disinvestment and the large foreign account deficit were depressing influences.

Perhaps the most notable developments were in the consumption sphere. Spurred by a fairly large increase in disposable personal income, which in turn could be traced to a 20 percent increase in transfer payments and the tax reductions made under the 1969 Tax Reform Act, consumption spending rose by 7.7 percent. But strong as this rise was, it was clearly held back by the continuation of the abnormally high rate of saving that had persisted since mid-1969.

Performance on the price side was again proving to be less satisfactory than hoped. After the early signs that inflation was beginning to decelerate, the evidence became mixed in the second quarter and revived concern about inflation. The CPI and the important industrial component of the WPI began to rise more rapidly in the spring, although the rate of increase of the GNP deflator (and its private component) showed a weak tendency to decline. The behavior of prices after the freeze is, of course, clouded by the impact of the freeze.

Though progress had been excruciatingly slow under its original economic game plan, it seems likely that the Nixon administration would have followed the course charted in 1969, at least until the end of 1971. However, events during the summer, culminating in the massive run on the dollar in early August, forced the administration to take drastic steps. The most important of these were the 90-day freeze on wages and prices and the suspension of convertibility of the dollar into gold, which eventually was translated into currency realignment. The fiscal measures that accompanied the freeze, which are of most interest in the present discussion, are discussed below. But first, let us consider briefly the freeze and its purpose.

From the time it came into power in 1969, the Nixon administration had disavowed the use of any kind of incomes policy, holding steadfastly to the belief that intentionally induced softness in the economy would produce backpressures on wages and prices that would eventually lead to acceptable price performance, and without creating a severe rise in the unemployment rate. Why, then, did the administration include the wage-price freeze in its actions of August 1971? The following seems to be a reasonable explanation.

Two-and-a-half years of experience with gradualism seemed to be suggesting strongly that inflation could not be squeezed out of the economy as quickly, easily, and painlessly as had been thought. Economic softness had produced substantial unemployment and should have produced the backpressures on wages and prices that the administration sought. But there was little relief in terms of less rapidly rising wages and prices. Backpressures or not, firms and unions with enough economic power to do so were making up for losses in real incomes that had resulted from unanticipated inflation. Moreover, after five years of inflation Americans seemed to have come to expect it and were acting to guard themselves from now-anticipated future losses in purchasing power. They could not easily be talked out of their inflationary expectations by administration officials speaking about "the other side of the valley." Thus the logical actions of firms, unions, and households that expected inflation made the inflationary expectations self-fulfilling. Finally, it seemed that consumers were losing confidence as they saw both prices and the unemployment rate continue to rise and were holding back on consumption spending, thereby aggravating the unemployment problem.[14]

---

[14] Usually it is thought that the anticipation of increased inflation would cause consumption to rise, rather than to fall. But if the unemployment rate is also

If this scenario describes the problems underlying the simultaneous existence of inflation and unemployment, then the freeze was a reasonable policy response. The administration apparently thought that the freeze would stop, at least for a while, the mad rush to raise prices and wages to catch up with past inflation and anticipate future inflation. The respite from wage increases would result in a less rapid increase in unit labor costs and make possible a slower rate of increase in prices once the freeze was lifted. On the other hand, both the appearance that something was being done to stop the inflation and evidence that prices were indeed rising less rapidly might be expected to lead to the modification of union demands. This, plus the slower rate of increase in prices of intermediate goods, would have further salutary effects on the rate of price increase in the economy. In this way the inflationary psychology could be broken and the inflationary spiral unwound. Finally, the freeze and the other components of the August New Economic Policy might restore consumer confidence. As evidence that this is the line of thought followed by the administration, we can quote the following passages from the CEA's annual report for 1972:

> If excess demand is avoided, the control system can help to break the habitual or contractual repetition of large price and wage increases that keeps inflation going. It can generate the *expectation* of reasonable price stability that is essential to the *achievement* of reasonable price stability. . . . Perhaps the most significant effect of the combined package was the impact on public confidence.[15]

Fiscal Elements of NEP. The fiscal components of the new economic plan were designed ostensibly to stimulate the economy in the short run while minimizing the loss of revenue in the longer run. The most important of the stimulative fiscal components of the New Economic Policy were the following:

1. The job development credit of 10 percent in the first year and

---

rising, households may become sufficiently uncertain of their economic position to want to increase their rate of saving. Similarly, continued deterioration of the purchasing power of income might induce sufficient uncertainty to cause a rise in the saving rate. For a further discussion of these issues, see F. Thomas Juster and Paul Wachtel, "Inflation and the Consumer," *Brookings Papers on Economic Activity*, 1: 1972 (Washington, D. C.: The Brookings Institution, 1972), pp. 71-114, and "A Note on Inflation and the Saving Rate," *Brookings Papers on Economic Activity*, 3: 1972 (Washington, D. C.: The Brookings Institution, 1972), pp. 765-778.

[15] *Annual Report of the Council of Economic Advisers*, 1972, pp. 27, 29 (emphasis in original).

5 percent thereafter would stimulate investment, especially in the first year after its enactment.

2. The repeal of the 7 percent excise tax on automobiles, which had been scheduled for 1966 but then set aside to help finance the Vietnam War, was expected to stimulate purchases of automobiles.

3. Earlier effective dates for two provisions of the 1969 Tax Reform Act would stimulate the economy in 1972 (and even late 1971) without reducing revenues after that. These were the increase in the personal exemption to $750 and the increase in the standard deduction to 15 percent of adjusted gross income, up to $2,000, originally scheduled for January 1, 1973, but proposed by Nixon to be made effective a year earlier.

4. Provision for special tax treatment of the Domestic International Sales Corporation (DISC) would stimulate exports.

5. The temporary 10 percent surcharge on dutiable imports (equivalent to a rate of 4.8 percent on all imports) was intended to provide protection for U.S. industries and probably for use as a bargaining ploy. Though this surcharge would raise revenue, its primary purpose and effect would be stimulative, rather than restrictive.

The remaining proposals in the fiscal sphere would have reduced expenditures, rather than increased them, and seem to have been included in the list primarily for public relations or simply as window dressing:

1. The clearest case of window dressing is the reduction in the estimate of fiscal 1972 outlays to take account of the delay in the passage of proposed legislation, especially for general and special revenue sharing and for welfare reform. Failure to follow the administration timetable for the enactment of proposed programs would certainly reduce projected expenditures and should be recognized in forecasts of economic conditions. But it seems rather far fetched to include as part of the New Economic Policy the results of congressional inaction on programs assigned a high priority by the President. Moreover, even if one were willing to count the effect of legislative delays as part of the new economic plan, he would still have to acknowledge that the delays being recognized constituted a perverse element in the new economic plan, running directly counter to the need for short-term stimulus!

2. The federal pay increase scheduled for January 1, 1972, was to be postponed for six months. Such a delay would offset part of the stimulus generated on the tax side, but was probably an essential part of the Nixon package if wages and salaries in the private sector were to be frozen.

3. The proposed 5 percent reduction in federal employment and the "miscellaneous small reductions in expenditures" seem to have no similar justification. Whether or not they made good sense in the long run, these spending cuts certainly constituted perverse fiscal policy in the short run. Thus on stabilization grounds it is difficult to understand their inclusion. The cryptic remark that the cut in federal employment "would be the most effective way to reduce Federal outlays with minimum short-range loss of service to the citizens" is of no help in understanding this proposal, since it is not clear why reducing federal outlays should be included as part of a stimulative fiscal package. One explanation would be simply that the administration wanted to fool a fiscally unsophisticated public by giving the impression that the government was sharing in the belt-tightening of the freeze, without bothering to note that the government's belt-tightening constituted restrictive fiscal policy. A more charitable and more sophisticated justification would be that the administration wanted both to achieve balance in the full-employment budget and hold down the size of the government on the one hand and to stimulate the economy on the other. This might be done by a careful choice of tax reductions (or even increases, in the case of the import surcharge) that had a large "bang for the buck" to combine with spending reductions of equal budgetary magnitude. That this might have been the goal is suggested by the choice of the tax reductions actually proposed and the assertion that "the program was intended and expected to be expansionary," even though it would reduce expenditures in fiscal 1972 by $1.1 billion more than it reduced receipts.[16]

As passed, the fiscal elements of the new economic plan were slightly less stimulative than proposed. (The revenue loss for calendar 1972 was $1.2 billion less than the administration's request.) However, the administration stated that this should not jeopardize the strong recovery which the new economic plan, including the tax bill, was expected to generate.[17]

Monetary policy during the second half of 1971 was distinctly restrictive, as there was almost no growth in the money supply from July to December. This seems to have been the result of an overestimate of the growth in the money supply implied by the market conditions upon which the Federal Reserve was basing monetary policy.

---

[16] The description of the fiscal components of the new economic plan—though not their interpretation—and the quotations are from *Annual Report of the Council of Economic Advisers*, 1972, pp. 69-70.

[17] Ibid., pp. 71-72.

Part of the expected expansive influence of fiscal policy in 1972 could be measured in terms of the 13 percent increase in federal expenditures (NIA basis) over their 1971 level. Alternatively, components of the increase could be examined. Federal purchases were budgeted to rise by 9 percent and state and local purchases by 12 percent, reflecting in part the stimulus expected to be provided by revenue sharing. Taxes would have fallen by $8.9 billion due to changes in tax law, but all but $3.7 billion of this amount was offset by a rise in the social security wage base. However, it was expected that the rise in the wage base and social security taxes would not strongly affect consumption during 1972. Finally, on a full-employment basis it was estimated that the unified budget would be in deficit by $8.1 billion in fiscal 1972 and move to balance in fiscal 1973, after having been in surplus by $4.9 billion in fiscal 1971.[18]

The Record for 1972. The preliminary figures for the 1971 national accounts showed that the skepticism that had met the CEA's now notorious $1,065 billion forecast for GNP had been well placed. Though the official figure was later revised to $1,050 billion, the initial estimate was that GNP for the year had amounted to only $1,047 billion, well below the council's forecast, but squarely in the middle of the range covered by private forecasters.

The official forecast for 1972 was near the middle of the closely bunched forecasts made outside the government. GNP, the council predicted, would rise by 9½ percent, or about $100 billion, to $1,145 billion. This gain, according to the official administration forecast, would be broken down into an increase in real GNP of about 6 percent and inflation of about 3¼ percent, as measured by the GNP deflator; and by the end of the year the unemployment rate should have fallen to about 5 percent and the rate of inflation to 2 to 3 percent.[19] While most private forecasters felt that the administration was overly optimistic in its allocation of the expected GNP increase between real output and inflation components, there was little disagreement with the prognosis that 1972 would be a good year.

The strong expansion was expected to be broad-based. Business-fixed investment was expected to rise by 8 percent over its 1971 level. Although the rise was not expected to be strong in the manufacturing sector, due to the still relatively low levels of plant utilization, extremely strong investment demands were expected in other sectors, especially airlines, electric and gas utilities, and communications.

---

[18] Ibid., pp. 104-106.
[19] Ibid., pp. 101, 108.

Profits, and with them retained earnings, would be increasing during the year, so that financing this level of investment should pose no problem, especially when account was taken of the newly enacted investment tax credit.

The second component of private investment, inventory accumulation, was also expected to contribute strongly to expansion, rising to $8 billion, after averaging barely $2 billion during the previous two years. Finally, total outlays for residential construction during 1972 were expected to rise by 15 percent, reflecting in part a substantial shift in housing starts from multi-family to single-family units. This forecast was based upon the belief that monetary policy would be more expansionary than it had been in the second half of 1971 and that, as a result, conditions in mortgage markets would not be such as to choke off the projected level of homebuilding.

Consumer spending was expected to rise by about 8 percent in 1972. This expansion would result primarily from increased disposable income originating in tax reductions and increased social security payments on the one hand and from the simple working of the multiplier process and the rise in other components of aggregate demand on the other. Even though the Council of Economic Advisers reported that consumer confidence had improved since the freeze and might improve still further, it was unwilling to base its forecasts for 1972 on the assumption that the high rate of saving out of disposable income would return to its historically lower level.[20]

In his 1971 economic report, President Nixon had suggested that "1971 will be a better year, leading to a good year in 1972." [21] He was just barely correct about 1971. But for 1972, when it really mattered politically, he was quite right. GNP rose by just over the $100 billion projected in the council's 1972 annual report, to $1,152 billion.[22] This 9½ percent rise in GNP consisted of a 6½ percent increase in real output and of only a 3.0 percent rise in the deflator. Thus for the first time since the Nixon team took command in 1969, the economy had performed better in terms of both prices and real output than had been predicted at the first of the year.

With the continued exception of net exports, which did not respond quickly to the devaluation of December 1971, all sectors of final demand contributed to the expansion. Benefiting from liberal-

---

[20] Ibid., p. 105.

[21] *Economic Report of the President*, 1971, p. 3.

[22] The rise of $101.7 billion was from a base of $1,050.4 billion, rather than from the preliminary figure for 1971 GNP of $1,046.8 billion used in preparing the 1972 *Annual Report of the Council of Economic Advisers*.

ized regulations governing depreciation allowances and the job development credit, the excise tax cuts on motor vehicles, the strong growth in aggregate demand during the year, and the ample availability of funds from both internal sources and capital markets, business-fixed investment rose by 14 percent from its 1971 level, compared with the expected 8 percent rise. Even greater in percentage terms was the rise of 26½ percent in residential construction. This reflected demographic factors, favorable conditions in mortgage markets, and the remaining legacy of inadequate homebuilding during the periods of tight money in the late 1960s. Particularly notable in this context was the execution of monetary policy. The Federal Reserve adopted as an additional target for day-to-day operations a particular rate of growth of reserves available to support private nonbank deposits. This seems to have resulted in a steadier rate of growth of the money supply than attention to market conditions alone had produced. The quarterly increases in the money supply were fairly closely bunched about the 8.7 percent rate for the year as a whole, ranging from 5.4 percent to 9.6 percent.

Of particular interest was the growth of consumption spending during 1972. The historically large 8½ percent increase in consumption occurred in the face of substantial overwithholding (roughly $9 billion) of the personal income tax.[23] Whereas personal income rose by 8.6 percent over its 1971 level, disposable income rose by only 6.8 percent, due to overwithholding. That consumption spending could rise by 8½ percent was made possible by the drop in the saving rate out of disposable personal income from 8.2 percent in 1971 to 6.9 percent in 1972. Stated differently, personal outlays as a percent of personal income were little changed from 1971, the increased percentage of personal income represented by personal taxes having been reflected in a fall in the rate of saving out of personal income.[24]

Several explanations for the drop in the saving rate are possible. The saving rate could simply have begun to fall toward its historical level as consumer confidence was restored. If this is the proper

---

[23] Overwithholding resulted from the attempt to adjust the withholding tables so that families with more than one source of labor income would not find at the end of the year that too little had been withheld, as happened in 1971. But under the new schedules, unrelated individuals and families with more than one source of labor income could avoid overwithholding only by claiming additional exemptions. Because most families with one source of labor income did not exercise the option to reduce their withholding taxes, overwithholding occurred in 1972 and abnormally large refunds were paid in 1973. This explanation is from *Annual Report of the Council of Economic Advisers*, 1973, p. 43.

[24] *Annual Report of the Council of Economic Advisers*, 1972, pp. 23-24.

explanation, the saving rate should remain below 7 percent during 1973 (barring further shocks) and could even fall a bit more. Alternatively, the decline in the saving rate might simply be a manifestation of the permanent income hypothesis. Under that hypothesis, which must be considered especially seriously in discussions of fiscal policy after the experience with the 1968 surcharge, consumers reduced saving, rather than spending, during 1972, in response to overwithholding, realizing that they could use refunds in early 1973 to achieve their saving objectives. If this is the correct explanation of events in 1972 the saving rate out of disposable income could be expected to rise to a very high level in early 1973 as refunds are paid to households (again, barring further disturbances).

Knowing which of these explanations is correct is both important and difficult. The importance lies in our desire to appraise the conduct of fiscal policy. If increased consumer confidence would have led to the fall in the saving rate that in fact occurred, independently of the overwithholding, and if the excess taxes impinged on consumption, then we can judge the overwithholding to have been a potentially harmful error, coming as it did when stimulus was needed. More important, the offsetting refunds during the first half of 1973 should have increased consumer spending, providing some stimulus that was not particularly welcome. If, on the other hand, the drop in the saving rate simply reflects the response of consumers to a tax change known to be temporary, as the permanent income hypothesis suggests, then the excess withholding may have been bothersome, but it represents no great error in fiscal policy. Nor could the 1973 refunds pose any serious problem, as they would have little impact on spending.

Knowing which explanation (or mix of explanations) is correct is difficult because there are so many other things happening concurrently. Even after data for the first half of 1973 are available we are unlikely to be able to determine why consumption held up so well in the face of overwithholding in 1972. But the 6.7 percent savings rate for the first quarter of 1973 suggests that it was the restoration of consumer confidence, and not the workings of the permanent income hypothesis, that caused the large increase in consumer spending in 1972, despite overwithholding.[25] Moreover, on a priori grounds it seems reasonable to attribute the 1972 performance to an unsteady

---

[25] Though one should not try to make too much of quarterly movements, the pattern of saving rates over the eight quarters ending with the first quarter of 1973 (8.6, 8.1, 7.8, 7.2, 6.4, 6.4, 7.5, and 6.7) could be interpreted as reflecting an improvement in consumer confidence.

start of the saving rate toward its historical average, rather than simply to the permanent income hypothesis. This is especially true since it seems unlikely that overwithholding, in spite of the attention it received in the press, had anywhere near the public recognition that the transitory nature of the 1968 surcharge had.

Total federal outlays rose by $26 billion, or 12 percent in 1972, somewhat less than the budgeted 13 percent. The $2.7 billion shortfall was produced by several events. First, because of delays in the passage of general revenue sharing, grant payments of $5.2 billion were made only in December 1972 and January 1973, rather than entirely in 1972 as originally budgeted. On the other hand, the first payments under the 20 percent increase in social security benefits increased 1972 outlays relative to budgeted levels. Finally, purchases fell somewhat short of anticipated levels, especially in the second half of the year.

Federal receipts for 1972 rose by $29 billion, or $13 billion more than budgeted. Nine billion dollars of this unbudgeted amount was, of course, due to overwithholding. As an offset, the postponement of the increase in the base for social security contributions to $10,200 until the beginning of 1973 reduced collections by some $2 billion. Finally, tax accruals ran somewhat ahead of what was foreseen at the start of the year.

Federal fiscal policy during 1972 was expansionary. Whereas the full-employment (NIA) budget showed a surplus of $1 billion in 1971, it showed a $4 billion deficit in 1972, due to increased expenditures and tax reductions.[26] Even this 1972 figure, the Council of Economic Advisers said, would understate the stimulus provided by the budget, since some of the $9 billion in overwithheld personal income taxes could be expected to have come out of savings, rather than consumption. While we can not know exactly how overwithholding affects saving and consumption, the council's attribution of

---

[26] Inexplicably, the council insists on using both NIA and unified budget concepts in reporting the balance of the full-employment budget. For example, in its 1973 annual report it uses NIA concepts on pages 40-43 but on page 74 speaks of "a shift of the budget—from a position in which the unified budget would be in deficit at full employment to a position in which it would be in balance at full employment." Perhaps the administration continues to use both concepts because it believes that fiscal discipline is most accurately measured by the balance of the unified budget (at full employment), but most fiscal analysts prefer to use the NIA basis. Even this is not stated explicitly. Since the differences in the two budgets must be quite incomprehensible to the layman and can be reconciled by specialists only after considerable effort, it seems reasonable to expect that either the council use only one of the concepts or that it provide quarterly data under each of the concepts and a reconciliation.

virtually all the impact to saving seems extreme.[27] Finally, state and local purchases rose by 10 percent in 1972, which was somewhat less than expected, due in part perhaps to the delayed passage of revenue sharing.[28]

The Prospects for 1973. The 1973 *Annual Report of the Council of Economic Advisers* forecasts that GNP for the year will rise from its 1972 level of $1,152 billion to about $1,267 billion. This 10 percent increase in GNP is well within the range covered by private forecasts, and was expected by the council to be split roughly into a 6¾ percent increase in real output and an increase in the GNP deflator of about 3 percent. An increase in GNP of this magnitude and composition, it was predicted, would result in a fall in the unemployment rate to about 4½ percent and a decline in the rate of inflation to 2½ percent or less by the end of the year.[29]

Fuel for this continued expansion was expected to come from the same sources as in 1972. For much the same reasons as in 1972, business-fixed investment was expected to match its 14 percent increase of the previous year. Inventory accumulation was expected to proceed at a substantially greater pace than in 1972, due in part to the low ratio of stocks to sales in important sectors of the economy and in part to the increase in work in process on heavy equipment with long production lead times. Of the major investment categories, only residential construction was expected to show little strength in 1973. But while homebuilding will fall in real terms, the drop was not expected to be dramatic.

State and local governments were expected to be a stimulative force, both directly and indirectly. Their purchases were expected to rise by 12 percent, reflecting in part the effects of revenue sharing.

---

[27] *Annual Report of the Council of Economic Advisers*, 1972, pp. 40-43. One can argue that unless a full-scale effort is made to produce a "weighted full-employment budget," it is best simply to report the full-employment estimates without adjustment. And yet, more information is better than less.

[28] A new element of uncertainty has been injected into the fiscal policy sphere. The advent of revenue sharing and demographic factors have combined to ease the fiscal pressure on state and local governments. How those governments respond to the prospect of surpluses will have important implications for the conduct of stabilization policy at the federal level; see *Annual Report of the Council of Economic Advisers*, 1973, pp. 44, 45. One of the first published recognitions of the easing of the fiscal crisis at the state and local level and the resulting paradox in the timing of the passage of revenue sharing was David J. Ott, Lawrence J. Korb, Thomas Gale Moore, Attiat F. Ott, Rudolph G. Penner, and Thomas Vasquez, *Nixon, McGovern and the Federal Budget* (Washington, D. C.: American Enterprise Institute, 1972), especially pp. 22-25.

[29] *Annual Report of the Council of Economic Advisers*, 1973, p. 82.

Revenue sharing may also result in lower taxes and higher private expenditures than would otherwise have occurred. Finally, because much of revenue sharing is likely to flow into capital projects, the initial impact will be recorded in inventory investment in the private sector.[30]

Federal fiscal policy during the year is seen as returning the unified budget to approximate balance at full employment.[31] Federal purchases will grow little between 1972 and 1973, but transfer payments and grants-in-aid to state and local governments will rise by significant amounts, due to higher social security benefits and increased payments for revenue sharing. The slow growth of federal expenditures reflects the administration's desire to hold expenditures within the limits posed by receipts at full employment. In an innovation introduced in the 1974 federal budget, it is estimated that even if substantial cuts are made in existing programs, expenditures for existing and proposed programs will virtually exhaust full-employment revenues (unified basis) in fiscal 1975.[32] Five billion dollars of the rise in full-employment receipts will be attributable to increases in the social security tax rates and wage base. For its part, monetary policy is expected to be somewhat less expansionary than in 1972, reflecting the changing needs of policy.

Consumer expenditures will again be a strongly expansionary force. Increases in social security payments in the last quarter of 1972 and during 1973 and the federal pay raise of $2.2 billion, as well

---

[30] *Annual Report of the Council of Economic Advisers,* 1973, pp. 82-85.

[31] No statement was made as to whether receipts in such a balanced budget reflect refunds for the personal income taxes overwithheld in 1972. If they do, then the budget would show a substantial surplus on a longer run basis. And it would be a restrictive influence even in the short run if the refunds flow primarily into saving, as the CEA seems to expect.

[32] *The Budget of the United States Government: Fiscal Year 1974* (Washington, D. C.: U.S. Government Printing Office, 1973), pp. 4-5, 38-49. References to disposal of materials from government stockpiles and the sale of loan and mortgage paper, adjustments in the timing of disbursements, et cetera, give the distinct impression that the administration was primarily interested in the *appearance* of a budget total for fiscal 1973 of less than $250 billion. While such a forthright admission of window dressing is refreshing, even if unintentional, it is nonetheless puzzling. Other budgetary projections that showed difficulties in holding expenditures to the level of full-employment receipts appear in Ott et al., *Nixon, McGovern and the Federal Budget,* and Charles L. Schultze, Edward R. Fried, Alice M. Rivlin, and Nancy H. Teeters, *Setting National Priorities: The 1973 Budget* (Washington, D. C.: The Brookings Institution, 1972), pp. 410-422. More recent projections by Ott et al., reflecting the budget-cutting efforts of the Nixon administration, show approximate balance in the full-employment budget (NIA) in 1975 and surplus after that. See David J. Ott et al., *Public Claims on U.S. Output: Federal Budget Options in the Last Half of the Seventies* (Washington, D. C.: American Enterprise Institute, forthcoming).

as the continued strength of the economy, will provide a strong impetus for consumer spending. Partly offsetting this will be the higher social security taxes that result from the increased rates and higher wage base. But the CEA expects the offset due to the higher wage base to be relatively minor, as the resulting increase in taxes does not start to affect take-home pay strongly until late in the year. Finally, some stimulus was expected to result from the refunds of personal income taxes overwithheld in 1972, though the CEA expects most of the refunds to flow into higher savings, rather than consumption.[33]

There can be little doubt that 1973 will be a good year. The Council of Economic Advisers is now estimating a year-to-year rise in GNP of a little over 11 percent, the bulk of the roughly 1 percent upward revision in the forecast being in the rate of inflation.[34] Indeed, the strength of the present expansion suggests that unless extreme caution is exercised, we may have moved far back into the area of excess aggregate demand by the end of the year.[35] If that occurs, we will see little progress on the inflation front and will be risking another recessionary period of cooling off.

In any event, we will be nearing the full-employment growth path. As that path is approached, we must try to determine with increased precision just where the path lies, we must try to improve the trade-offs between inflation and unemployment, and we must remain vigilant lest we are thrown off that path by inappropriate monetary and fiscal policies. This essay is not the place to discuss either what level of unemployment should be defined as full employment or how we can reconcile lower levels of employment with satisfactory price performance. But it does seem worthwhile at this point to appraise the exercise of fiscal policy under the Nixon

---

[33] *Annual Report of the Council of Economic Advisers*, 1973, p. 86. It is interesting to note that the council apparently thinks that consumers will have adjusted their saving rates to even out the fluctuations in consumption spending that would otherwise have resulted from overwithholding in 1972 but that consumers will not reduce consumption in response to the portion of higher social security taxes that can be attributed to the increase in the wage base until the taxes are reflected in lower take-home pay. Why is not clear.

[34] Herbert Stein, excerpts of remarks to the 26th Annual Conference of the Financial Analysts Federation, Washington, D. C., May 7, 1973, p. 2.

[35] See Roger W. Spencer, "Business Recovery Continues," *Review* of the Federal Reserve Bank of St. Louis, vol. 54 (December 1972), pp. 2-10, for a comparison of the present recovery with the average of the three postwar recoveries. Whereas on the average the earlier recoveries started fast and then faltered (except the recovery that began in 1961), the present recovery started slowly and then accelerated.

administration and discuss briefly how fiscal policy can be improved. The concluding section is devoted to these questions.

But it would not be proper to fail to note at least one important issue that cannot be ignored. If 4½ or 5 percent is adopted as the new goal of employment policy because of shifts in the composition of the labor force, it makes little sense to continue to call the budget standardized for a 4 percent unemployment rate the "full-employment budget." It has been estimated that standardized for a 5 percent unemployment rate, the full-employment budget for fiscal 1972 would show a deficit of $23.5 billion, rather than $8.1 billion.[36] Thus the administration faces a frustrating dilemma. If it continues to view 4 percent as full employment, policies of the type followed in late 1970 and early 1971 can be criticized as overly restrictive, as they resulted in relatively large full-employment surpluses at a time of substantial unemployment. Redefinition of full employment to 4½ or 5 percent would result in a picture of a much more stimulative fiscal policy and a more acceptable performance on the employment front. Thus it would be harder to fault the fiscal policy pursued in 1970-71 and easier for the administration to make the point that at present fiscal policy is much too stimulative.[37] But whether or not such a redefinition of full employment is sensible on objective grounds, it would entail considerable political expense. In what follows we assume that the now traditional goal of a 4 percent unemployment rate has not been abandoned.

Nixon's Fiscal Policy Appraised

There can be little doubt that the original Nixon policy for stabilization was largely unsuccessful, if only in its timing. The CEA's annual report for 1970 describes clearly the game plan of gradualism as it was seen in early 1969: Policy would induce a slowdown in the growth of spending, a decline in the rate of growth of production, a decline in profits per unit, a slowdown in wage increases, and a slowdown in price increases. Once economic softness and backpressures on wages and prices had been established, restimulation would put the economy back on the path of full employment and a satisfactory

[36] See Edgar L. Feige in "The 1972 Report of the President's Council of Economic Advisers: Inflation and Unemployment," *American Economic Review*, September 1972, p. 513.

[37] Not enough has been made of this important point, though it has been mentioned by Fellner in Cagan et al., *Economic Policy and Inflation in the Sixties*, pp. 2-3, and by Murray L. Weidenbaum, Dan Larkins, and Philip N. Marcus, *Matching Needs and Resources: Reforming the Federal Budget* (Washington, D. C.: American Enterprise Institute, 1973), p. 1, for example.

performance of wages and prices. Though the council was too cautious to set a timetable—and rightfully so—one can infer that it expected the process of disinflation and restimulation to last not much longer than one year, and no more than two years, at the longest. This is suggested by the words chosen to describe policies for 1970 (after those same policies had produced the expected results only very slowly in 1969):

> Despite the uncertainties of degree, it does seem likely that by mid-1970 the economy, after three quarters of very little increase in real output, would be producing significantly below its potential. Such a GNP gap places a downward pressure on the rate of inflation. . . . These pressures against inflation will continue if demand remains below potential output, even though demand begins to rise more rapidly.
> Thus, in the second half of 1970 a moderately more rapid rise of money demand, bringing about an increase of real output, would be consistent with a further reduction of the rate of inflation.
> The exact timing and degree of expansion that would be consistent with a significant reduction in inflation in 1970 are uncertain. However, it seems a reasonable estimate that the slow increases of GNP foreseeable in the first half plus the moderately larger but still non-inflationary increases desirable in the second half would add up to a GNP for the year between $980 and $990 billion.[38]

Of course, the council did not expect the economy to return to its potential output immediately. In another part of its report, it wrote: "Projected available output is assumed to be below potential from 1970 until 1972, as a result of policies to slow inflation." [39] But it also did not expect the unemployment rate to rise as much as it did or to stay high for as long as it has. Thus Chairman Paul McCracken told the Joint Economic Committee of the Congress in February 1970 that the unemployment rate would average no more than 4.3 percent for the year as a whole.

Despite the failure of the economy to respond as predicted during 1970, the Nixon administration continued into 1971 to pursue the policies it had announced in 1969. These, it asserted, would pro-

---

[38] *Annual Report of the Council of Economic Advisers*, 1970, p. 58.

[39] *Annual Report of the Council of Economic Advisers*, 1970, p. 79. Though the use of "until 1972" and "to 1972" leaves considerable (and probably intentional) ambiguity, the chart on page 85 of the annual report suggests that actual GNP would reach potential GNP only toward the end of 1972.

duce an unemployment rate of about 4½ percent and a rate of inflation of about 3 percent by mid-1972. When little relief was seen on either the inflation or the unemployment side by early August, the administration reversed its field and imposed a ninety-day freeze on prices and wages and increased the fiscal stimulus to the economy.

In retrospect, it seems unfortunate that President Nixon waited for two-and-one-half years before turning to some form of incomes policy, since the case for such a policy was as strong (though not as obvious) during much of that period as it was in August 1971. It is doubly unfortunate that he announced early in 1969 that he would not resort to wage-price controls, guidelines, or jawboning. Over most of the first two-and-one-half years of the Nixon administration the economy was very soft—as it was intended to be. Yet wages and prices did not respond as expected, because of the successful efforts of economically strong unions and firms to make up for past and guard against future inflation. The announcement of an incomes policy once the remnants of demand-pull inflation had been eliminated would have tended to check wage and price increases not justified by aggregate demand conditions. This, in turn, would probably have shortened the period of transition to a satisfactory wage-price performance and would have spared the nation much of the cost of being put through the wringer for so long to squeeze inflation and inflationary expectations out of the economy by conventional means alone. As it was, not only did President Nixon initially reject an incomes policy, but he also publicly disavowed any intention of ever interfering with private wage and price determination. This can only have added to inflationary expectations and made the subsequent adjustment longer and more difficult.

The 1970 recession resulted from the attempt to disinflate the economy after excess aggregate demand had been allowed to develop and cause inflation. Though the recession was relatively mild, it lasted longer and recovery from it was slower than had been hoped and expected. Much of the blame for the failure of the economy to recover more quickly can be attributed to an overly tight fiscal policy. The fiscal restraint begun with the 1968 surcharge and continued by the Nixon administration in 1969 was clearly required. But during 1970, when the economy was operating at well below its potential and the unemployment rate was rising rapidly toward the 6 percent level, the full-employment budget (NIA basis) showed a surplus of over $6½ billion. (Even if the $10.4 billion surplus in the first quarter is omitted, the average surplus for the year was almost $5½ billion.) [40]

_____

[40] *Annual Report of the Council of Economic Advisers*, 1971, p. 24.

And even this is well below the surplus of $10 billion that would have occurred if the administration had been able to make good on its budgetary promises of February 1970. Finally, for the first half of 1971, a period when the unemployment rate hovered near 6 percent, the full-employment surplus was a very high $8.2 billion.[41] Only after the middle of 1971, as part of the New Economic Policy, was the full-employment budget allowed to go into deficit on a national income accounts basis.[42]

The New Budgetary Orthodoxy. One can adduce several possible explanations for this kind of policy. First, the Nixon administration placed a high premium on halting inflation. Since it would not use more direct (incomes policy) means of dealing with inflation, it would have to allow the economy to run at below capacity for long enough to rid it of inflationary expectations. One way to assure the necessary economic softness was to pursue a restrictive fiscal policy, that is, to run a full-employment surplus, though full employment was nowhere in sight.

Second, the administration wanted to combine a slightly restrictive fiscal policy with a moderately expansionary monetary policy. Presumably the notion was that maintaining a given level of aggregate demand in this way, rather than through tight money and a looser fiscal policy, would allow the recovery of residential construction and state and local spending. Both because the question of the optimal *mix* of stabilization policies is a complicated one and because it can be argued that the *totality* of monetary and fiscal policy was too restrictive during 1970 and early 1971, it seems best to pursue this issue no further in this essay.[43]

The third reason for running a full employment surplus during 1970 and early 1971 seems to involve an article of faith—or, more accurately, several articles of faith. President Nixon and many of his key economic advisers dislike the growth of federal expenditures.[44]

---

[41] This is calculated from the figures for the second half of 1970 in *Annual Report of the Council of Economic Advisers*, 1971, p. 24 and those for fiscal 1971 in Nancy H. Teeters, "The 1973 Federal Budget," *Brookings Papers on Economic Activity*, 1: 1972 (Washington, D. C.: The Brookings Institution, 1972), p. 223.

[42] Teeters, ibid.

[43] See, however, the discussion in Okun, "Rules and Roles for Fiscal and Monetary Policy," in Diamond, ed., *Issues in Fiscal and Monetary Policy: The Eclectic Economist Views the Controversy*. For a provocative discussion of the issues involved in choosing the proper level of full-employment surplus, see Martin J. Bailey, "The Optimal Full-Employment Surplus," *Journal of Political Economy*, July-August 1972, pp. 649-661.

[44] One of the many places this is stated explicitly is in the *Annual Report of the Council of Economic Advisers*, 1973, pp. 76-78.

Moreover, and as a separate point, they fear the repetition of the kind of demand-pull inflationary binge that began in the mid-1960s with the failure to raise taxes to pay for the Vietnam War and the Great Society programs. Finally, they believe that success in the battle against both these evils depends at least in part upon budgetary discipline, that is, upon the matching of new expenditures with taxes to pay for them. Avoidance of demand-pull inflation resulting from budgetary deficits depends definitionally upon budgetary discipline. And if tax increases can be avoided, budgetary discipline also helps to hold down the growth of the federal sector.

Fortunately for the American public, the President—and with him the official policies of his administration—was converted, though slowly and rather haltingly, from the previous orthodoxy that the *actual budget* should be balanced at all times to the idea than balance in the *full-employment budget* should be the objective of policy. Unfortunately, "balance at full employment" almost immediately became a new orthodoxy. That is, the administration adopted a policy stance that expenditures should not exceed the receipts that would be collected at full employment, except in emergencies. And it clearly did not consider that conditions in 1970 and early 1971 qualified as an emergency. Thus, in the name of this new fiscal orthodoxy, the nation was subjected to a fiscal policy that was inappropriately tight for a time of high unemployment.

Ironically, the administration was adopting this new orthodoxy at just the time the Committee for Economic Development was urging that more flexibility be added to its classical prescription for a stabilizing budget. In January 1969 the CED, a very early proponent of the use of the full-employment budget as a measure of fiscal restraint and a stalwart advocate of approximate balance in the high employment budget, had come out publicly for the use of discretionary fiscal action when the economy strayed far from the full-employment growth path.[45]

---

[45] See *Fiscal and Monetary Policies for Steady Economic Growth.* Two more recent statements, *Further Weapons against Inflation* and *High Employment without Inflation* contain the latest policy views of the CED. For a similar personal view of Frank W. Schiff, chief economist for the CED, see "Control of Inflation and Recession," *Annals of the American Academy of Political and Social Science*, vol. 396 (July 1971), pp. 90-104. Schiff notes (p. 97) that "the importance which the rule attaches to what might happen once actual full employment is reached could in fact serve as a major obstacle toward getting there." Similarly, in testimony before the Joint Economic Committee on March 10, 1971, Emilio G. Collado, chairman of the Research and Policy Committee of the CED noted that because of the continued high rate of unemployment, the $6-$10 billion full-employment surplus proposed by the CED in November 1970 should be scaled down.

Politics and Fiscal Discipline. Another related article of faith is reminiscent of the original CED preference for a stabilizing budget and is doubtlessly attributable to Herbert Stein. In defense of "the principle of keeping expenditures that would be made at full employment within the level of receipts that would be yielded by the existing tax system under conditions of full employment," the Council of Economic Advisers noted that "a policy of ad hoc decisions about deficit or surplus is exposed to the political bias in favor of spending and deficits." It goes on to argue that

> the problems of managing fiscal or monetary policy or both have apparently been underestimated. . . . But if the question is not one of keeping the economy on a narrowly defined path but one of avoiding violent aberrations like the one that began in 1965, our tools are probably adequate, and the problem is more the national will than the techniques of economics and economic policy. [46]

Thus the new orthodoxy was based on a desire to resist the political bias toward deficits and inflation and a willingness to settle for "good" performance, rather than striving for a "best" performance that might be unattainable as a practical matter.[47]

A careful reading of the annual reports of the Nixon Council of Economic Advisers gives the distinct impression that the administration's fiscal policy was predicated on the new fiscal orthodoxy. At times, actual budget deficits were defended not by stating candidly that stimulus was needed, but by noting that expenditures would not exceed full-employment revenues. To be fair, there are compelling

---

[46] *Annual Report of the Council of Economic Advisers*, 1972, p. 112. In its 1971 annual report, p. 21, the council wrote: "We have not appreciably reduced the incidence of small departures from maximum employment but we have reduced the incidence of large departures, which is just what one would expect aggregate economic policy to be able to do."

[47] Okun has criticized the administration strongly for its adherence to a new orthodoxy in "Fiscal-Monetary Activism: Some Analytical Issues," *Brookings Papers on Economic Activity*, 1: 1972, pp. 123-163. In particular, he has questioned the propensity to break fiscal rules only if deviations from targets are large (pp. 152-154) and the assumption that fiscal rules are needed because policy makers cannot be trusted to act responsibly (pp. 154-157). While the author shares Okun's disapproval of the conduct of fiscal policy during the year before the freeze—and after it became apparent that the economy would not recover quickly (see Okun, "Rules and Roles for Fiscal and Monetary Policy," pp. 71-74)—he finds it rather strange that a member of the Council of Economic Advisers from late 1964 until early 1969 would remain a staunch defender of the rationality of political decisions on fiscal policy. That important goals other than stability may complicate the problem of maintaining stability is not enough, it seems, to excuse the political failures in the exercise of fiscal policy from early 1966 to mid-1968.

reasons—based upon an analysis of political realities—why it might have been worthwhile to maintain a full-employment surplus, even at the risk of imposing excessive fiscal restraint on the economy. These are not unrelated to the various articles of faith mentioned above.

Several studies had shown that expenditures for programs already in existence or proposed by the administration would more than exceed the revenues that the present tax system would yield at full employment until near the end of this decade.[48] This finding suggested that it might be difficult to prevent the recovery from the 1970 recession from taking the economy past the target path for GNP and back into the region of excess aggregate demand. Certainly, it might be necessary to slow the growth in existing programs, curtail proposed programs, or raise taxes if budgetary balance at full employment were to be maintained over the next few years.

Seen in this perspective, the full-employment surpluses of the Nixon administration during late 1970 and early 1971 begin to make more sense. If the intermediate to long-run prospect is for difficulty in limiting expenditure increases to the secular growth in full-employment receipts, it would be unwise from a long-run viewpoint to cut taxes or increase expenditures for short-run countercyclical reasons. This is especially true if, as the Council of Economic Advisers believed, the economic slowdown induced by a tight fiscal policy would be short and mild in any case. Only if taxes could be cut temporarily to stimulate the economy and then returned to their previous levels, so that their long-range revenue productivity would not be jeopardized, would it be clear that the restrictive Nixon budgets were unjustified.

But given present institutions, one could not reasonably assume that taxes, once cut, could or would be restored to their previous levels. Raising taxes is always more distasteful than lowering them and the administration had no faith that the Congress would bite the fiscal bullet when restraint was required; certainly, it had not done so in the period from early 1966 to mid-1968. Moreover, the restoration of taxes to their previous level could easily become the hostage of those seeking tax reform and therefore might be delayed in the Congress. And, substantive tax reform would probably prove to be unpopular with Republican supporters of the administration. In this way the case against a tax cut was compounded.

---

48 Ott et al., *Nixon, McGovern and the Federal Budget*, and Schultze et al., *Setting National Priorities*. The second of these provides an interesting analysis of how we have "spent" the fiscal dividends that the discussion of the 1964 tax cut led us to expect as a normal fact of life.

Clearly what was needed, once it became clear that recovery would be slower than expected, was a temporary tax reduction patterned after the 1968 surcharge. Such a "negative surcharge" could be made more or less distributionally neutral and would automatically vanish at a predetermined time, unless extended by legislation. Thus a protracted discussion of tax reform could be avoided. Much as the earlier passage of the 1968 surcharge would have helped to prevent inflation, timely enactment of a temporary tax reduction would have speeded recovery, without reducing revenues in the long run.

Why the administration did not ask even for a temporary tax cut is unclear. Most obviously, it had considerable faith that conventional policies of demand management already in place would halt inflation and allow a quick recovery, even without a tax cut. Not much time passed between the recognition that progress under gradualism was altogether too gradual and the initiation of the New Economic Policy. If events had not forced this new policy upon the administration, fiscal stimulus via a temporary tax reduction might eventually have been requested. As it was, the freeze was accompanied by requests for measures that would stimulate the economy in the short run without resulting in substantial revenue loss in the long run, as noted above.

Beyond the time question, the role played by the new fiscal orthodoxy undoubtedly exerted some influence, though how much may never be known. President Nixon may have been able to accept the notion that the actual budget need not be balanced so long as the full-employment budget was balanced, but not the idea that even the full-employment budget should be allowed to go into deficit in order to stimulate the economy. Or the CEA may simply not have suggested that stimulus was needed. This is especially likely in the light of what appears to be a basic error in economic analysis that appears in the following quotation from the council's annual report for 1971:

> The absolute level of the full-employment surplus or deficit is of limited significance for indicating how much restraint or stimulus the budget would exert on the economy if it followed the full-employment path, or indeed for indicating which of these directions its influence would take. Changes in the full-employment surplus from period to period are much more important indicators of how much fiscal policy is moving toward contraction or expansion. The fact that the full-employment budget has a surplus does

not imply that the budget is not having an expansionary impact on the economy; the effects may be expansionary if the surplus is declining. Similarly a budget with a deficit may be restrictive if the deficit is declining.[49]

According to this line of reasoning, the $5 billion drop in the full-employment surplus between 1969 and 1970 is seen as expansionary—despite the fact that the surplus only fell to $6.7 billion.[50] And, to carry this line of thought further, there would be no reason to cut taxes, given the shift in the budgetary position that had already occurred.

The error in this kind of reasoning hardly requires detailed explanation. Certainly the drop in the full-employment surplus means that the budget was less restrictive in 1970 than in 1969. But the implication that the budget was stimulative in 1970 is invalid. The *change* in the budget stance aside, the full-employment surplus in 1970 may have been so high as to preclude the attainment of full employment.[51]

Flexibility with Discipline. Experience with both excess aggregate demand and inadequate demand suggests that the President should be given discretionary power to raise or lower income taxes within predetermined limits and for set periods of time, subject to congressional veto. Alternatively, a new system of temporary taxes and subsidies on investment and consumer durable spending, to be introduced and varied at the President's discretion, could be introduced.[52] (Because of the inefficiencies involved, it does not seem wise to attempt countercyclical variations in most federal expenditures.) But even if one of these schemes were to be legislated, we cannot be sure that the economy would perform much better than it has. Giving the

---

[49] *Annual Report of the Council of Economic Advisers, 1971*, p. 72.

[50] Ibid., p. 24.

[51] One possible rationale for focusing upon the change in the full-employment budget balance, rather than the level of the balance, is the monetarist view that in the long run the balance is more-or-less irrelevant, the macroeconomic state of the economy depending primarily upon the rate of growth of the money supply. According to this view, changes in the full-employment budget balance are more important than levels because any change will have a short-run impact which will taper off in the long run as monetary influences come to dominate fiscal forces. Even granting the validity of this argument, there is nothing to suggest that the authors of the 1971 annual report had it in mind when they wrote the passage quoted above.

[52] For a discussion of the latter proposal, see McLure, *Fiscal Failure: Lessons of the Sixties.* One advantage of this approach is that it is less likely to be rendered ineffective by consumer behavior that conforms with the permanent income hypothesis than is an income tax surcharge.

President the power to levy positive and negative surcharges is not the same as commanding him to use that power, and use it wisely. Presumably President Johnson would have used the power in 1966, but we can not be sure, because of the growing unpopularity of the Vietnam War and the certainty that higher taxes would have increased the unpopularity. And President Nixon might not have cut taxes in 1970 or 1971. After all, his Council of Economic Advisers believed that softness was necessary to squeeze inflation out of the economy, that built-in stabilizers should bear the bulk of the burden in demand management, and that changes in the full-employment surplus were more important than levels as an indicator of fiscal restraint.

Because of the manifest risks of mismanagement of discretionary fiscal policy, some economists have recently supported strongly the old notion of formula flexibility. Under this scheme, certain key fiscal variables would rise and fall with the performance of the economy in order to stabilize output around some target growth path.[53] This is not the place to discuss formula flexibility in detail. But one must certainly concede that the economic performance of recent years can probably be improved and that formula flexibility deserves serious attention. It is worth emphasizing, however, that the design of the formulas by which tax rates and expenditures (especially unemployment compensation) would be varied is no simple matter. A carelessly designed system could be destabilizing (or stabilizing at the wrong level or path of output). Nor has anyone ever paid much attention to the administrative aspects of this theoretically attractive application of control theory to economic problems.

Moreover, one intriguing question that would arise under a scheme of formula flexibility (or if temporary positive and negative surcharges were used for stabilization purposes, for that matter) is how the full-employment surplus would be computed when the economy was far enough from its target path for taxes or expenditures to be changed temporarily by formula (or by discretion in the case of a temporary surcharge). It would not be consistent simply to calculate the full-employment surplus implied by the then existing pattern of taxes and expenditures, including temporary elements— because, by assumption, the attainment of full employment would result in the elimination of the temporary adjustments to taxes and expenditures resulting from formula flexibility (or discretionary, but temporary, surcharges). Yet some measure of the total macroeco-

[53] See for example, Arnold H. Packer and Frank C. Ripley, "The Design of a Self-stabilizing Economy," 1972 (xeroxed). An element of formula flexibility has recently been introduced into payments for unemployment compensation.

nomic stance of fiscal policy—including deliberately temporary elements—standardized for the level of employment would be needed. Perhaps the best that could, and should, be done would be to compute two measures of the full-employment budget. The first measure, which would be the primary focus of discussions of fiscal responsibility and discipline, would present a "long-run" or "normal" picture of how taxes and expenditures would compare at full employment. It would exclude any explicitly temporary changes in taxes and expenditures, and might be done on a unified budget basis. The second measure, which would be used primarily as an indication of the macroeconomic stance of fiscal policy, would include these temporary elements and might be on the NIA basis. The inconsistency mentioned above of calculating the full-employment budget balance based on tax rates and expenditure programs that would by law (or discretion) be different if full employment were actually achieved would pose relatively little problem if this dual approach to measurement were used. For the second purpose full employment would serve simply as a standard for measurement.

The final issue that deserves attention in this essay, but which can be given no more than passing mention, is the question of presidential impounding of funds. Fearing both the rise in the level of government spending and the threat that such higher spending will not be fully financed by higher taxes and will be inflationary, the President has refused to spend funds appropriated by Congress. For its part, the Congress, seeing the impounding of funds as an attempt by the President to usurp the financial prerogatives guaranteed to the Congress by the Constitution, questions the legality of the act. In rebuttal, the President asserts that if the Congress would put its own house in order and hold appropriations within the limits set by full-employment revenues, impounding would not be necessary.

In this debate there are no totally correct viewpoints and no totally incorrect ones.[54] We need go back no further than to the late 1960s to see the validity of the President's basic position. At that time, more was being spent than was being collected in taxes and, although much of the blame for this must rest with President Johnson, the Congress acted irresponsibly by neither raising taxes

---

[54] It does seem unlikely, however, that the President's acts are illegal or unconstitutional. Nancy H. Teeters cites several examples of impounding by Presidents Truman and Johnson and gives references to more detailed studies in "Outlook for Federal Fiscal Policy," *Brookings Papers on Economic Activity*, 2: 1972 (Washington, D. C.: The Brookings Institution, 1972), pp. 472-474. Certainly it does not appear likely that the present Supreme Court would find impounding unconstitutional.

nor holding down expenditures. Given that congressional decision making is no better now than it was then, the President seems to be quite right in trying to see that we do not repeat in the next few years the inflationary experience that is only now ending.

On the other hand, one can easily appreciate the position of the Congress. In the name of fiscal responsibility, the President has held the total level of spending to below what Congress appropriated. In doing so, he has cut the budget in areas of particular interest to certain members of the Congress, especially in areas of social legislation dear to many liberal legislators. In addition to the rather personal loss of power its members must feel, there is an important question of the balance of power between the legislative and executive branches of government. Congress appears to view any further shift of power to the White House as a potentially serious matter.

On balance, it seems as though the President has the better side in the current debate. The Congress examines the budget only on a piecemeal basis, never as a whole. Therefore the total amounts appropriated need bear no resemblance to full-employment revenues. Indeed, total outlays come up for congressional consideration only rarely. And even then the Congress has tended simply to set an expenditure ceiling below the total of appropriations, leaving to the White House the unpopular task of paring down outlays. Then when the paring has cut too close to home, the Congress has complained.[55]

At this point the burden of proof is on the Congress. Before it can legitimately criticize the administration for impounding funds it must set its own house in order by instituting procedures to ensure that, once full employment is reached, receipts will cover expenditures—even if this means raising taxes, cutting existing programs, or forgoing expenditure increases. Then and only then will it have a strong case against the impounding of funds and the assertion of White House priorities in decisions on how to spend the available revenues.

Concluding Remarks. In conclusion, it seems that we can make several judgments about the pursuit of fiscal policy under the Nixon administration that have important lessons for the future. First, the administration is no doubt correct that some rule must be adopted to guarantee long-run budgetary discipline in a situation of full employ-

---

[55] An interesting example is in the news as this is being written. Several senators who have consistently opposed high military spending are complaining bitterly about the closing of military installations in their states as part of the Pentagon's economy move.

ment. Such a rule would have prevented much of the inflationary experience that began with the fiscal irresponsibility of the late 1960s and it would prove helpful in restraining tendencies toward excess aggregate demand that are likely to develop in 1973 and beyond. But it should be a presumptive rule, not a dogma that would prevent the use of discretionary fiscal policy when the economy is far from the target path—which is what happened in late 1970 and early 1971. In order to reconcile budgetary discipline with flexible fiscal policy, it is necessary that we take measures to allow the imposition of temporary and self-terminating positive or negative surcharges on the income tax at the President's discretion. Alternatively, we might consider some uses of formula flexibility or the use of variable taxes or subsidies on investment and consumer durables. The important thing is that tax measures taken for countercyclical reasons should be temporary and self-terminating, and therefore not inconsistent with the important goal of rough balance in the budget when full employment is actually achieved. A presumptive rule that the full-employment budget should be in rough balance when the economy is at full employment, but perhaps not otherwise, has two important corollaries. The first is that congressional decision making on the budget must be improved so that budgetary discipline can be maintained. The second is that we should stand ready to use some form of incomes policy as a supplement to traditional policies of demand management in order to improve the trade-off between employment and inflation at less than full employment. We should not, of course, attempt to use an incomes policy as a substitute for responsible demand management in an environment in which excess aggregate demand is producing demand-pull inflation.

3

INTERNATIONAL ASPECTS
OF U.S. INFLATION*

Gottfried Haberler

*After a brief historical introduction, the development of the
U.S. balance of payments since August 1971 and the nature
of the recent currency crises are discussed in some detail.
The reasons for the chronic weakness of the dollar are
analyzed with special reference to the U.S. inflation. The
theory is examined that under the "dollar standard" the
United States sets the pace of inflation in those countries
that peg their currencies to the dollar. Special attention is
given to the divergence between consumer prices and
export prices in different countries. This divergence gives
rise to what is called "an inflation-transmission multiplier."
A postscript on events since May deals with the renewed
weakness of, and lack of confidence in, the dollar. What
has happened is best described as an appreciation of
some Western European currencies, especially the German
mark and the Swiss franc. Since floating became general
last March, the dollar has remained practically unchanged
in terms of the currencies of countries that account for
three-fourths of U.S. trade (that is, sterling, the Canadian
dollar, the lira, the yen and many less important ones).
It is argued that since the dollar is now probably undervalued, a case can be made for judicious interventions in
support of the dollar.*

Introduction

The adoption of a New Economic Policy on August 15, 1971 was
prompted to a large extent by the sharp deterioration in the U.S.

---

* Completed in May 1973. See Postscript: Developments Since Completion of
This Paper, page 99 below.

international payments position in early 1971 and by the ensuing speculation which, on May 9, had forced the floating of the German mark and the Dutch guilder and the appreciation of the Swiss franc and Austrian schilling. The previous year, 1970, had brought a slight improvement in the U.S. balance of payments. The surplus in the widely watched trade balance had risen from $0.6 billion for 1969 to $2.2 billion. Later in 1970 this surplus declined and in the second quarter of 1971 a large deficit of $3.6 billion (annual rate) suddenly developed.

The Smithsonian Agreement of December 18, 1971 brought a far-reaching realignment of parities. It provided for a depreciation of the dollar in terms of gold and SDRs of almost 8 percent, producing a devaluation in terms of the major currencies of about 7½ percent on a trade-weighted basis.

It was generally realized that devaluation would not improve the U.S. balance of payments quickly, but further deterioration in the trade balance in 1972—to a record deficit of $6.8 billion for the whole year—came as a shocking surprise. Thus on February 12, 1973, fourteen months after the Smithsonian conference, the dollar was again depreciated by 10 percent in terms of gold and SDRs, resulting in a trade-weighted devaluation of 6.5 percent in terms of fourteen major currencies.[1]

Before describing and analyzing these events in greater detail, it will be useful to put the recent developments into somewhat broader perspectives.

Historical Perspectives

During the first fifteen years after World War II the dollar ruled supreme in the world economy. The economies of Western Europe and Japan were shattered by the war and American industry had an unchallenged quasi-monopoly position. But with lavish American help, Europe and Japan recovered much more quickly than was generally thought possible. Germany's recovery started in 1948 when Ludwig Erhard put the German economy on the path of sustained rapid growth and prosperity by discarding wartime controls and by radically slashing the monetary overhang inherited from the war, thus giving Germany a sound monetary system.

---

[1] This figure is taken from *World Financial Markets* (New York: Morgan Guaranty Trust Company, February 23, 1973). The depreciation from the Smithsonian Agreement central rates was 6.05 percent. From the pre-June 1970 parities the trade-weighted depreciation against fourteen major currencies was 16.64 percent. (By the end of May the figure was about 18 percent.)

The German example, which Japan surpassed by using essentially the same type of policies, had a tremendous impact. It showed that the "classical medicine," [2] sound money and free enterprise, could still work if given a chance.

During the 1950s Europe and Japan managed to accumulate a substantial international reserve consisting of gold and dollars. While many well-known and influential economists, especially in Great Britain, spoke of a perpetual "dollar shortage," the U.S. had a small deficit of about $1 billion in each year from 1950 to 1956. In 1957, the year of the Suez crisis, the U.S. had its last small surplus. Then in 1958, 1959, and 1960, a series of large deficits appeared—$3.4 billion, $3.9 billion, and $3.7 billion, respectively. [3]

These deficits caused great concern. They greatly contributed to the decision of the Eisenhower administration to take energetic anti-inflationary measures on the fiscal and monetary front. The anti-inflation policy produced a mild recession from May 1960 to February 1961 and laid the foundation for the remarkable stability of prices that lasted until 1965. The trade balance improved from a surplus of $1.1 billion in 1959 to one of $5.6 billion in 1964 and the surplus in the balance of goods and services rose from $0.3 billion to $8.6 billion.

In 1965 inflation started again when the Johnson administration began to finance the escalating war in Vietnam and rising Great Society expenditures by borrowing and inflating rather than by higher taxes. Actually, in 1964, taxes had been reduced and the rate of increase in the money supply had quickly accelerated. [4] The export surplus fell to a low level in the fourth quarter of 1968. In that quarter and the first half of 1969 the trade balance was slightly in the red. It improved somewhat in the second half of 1969 and 1970 but, as mentioned earlier, it then fell deeply into the red in the first half of 1971 and has not yet recovered. The balance of

---

[2] These words are Keynes' in his famous posthumously published paper "The Balance of Payments of the United States," in which he castigated his radical followers, calling their writings "modernist stuff gone wrong and turned silly and sour." (*The Economic Journal*, June 1946, p. 186).

[3] These figures relate to the so-called "liquidity" definition then in general use as the measure of imbalance. Under that concept, a deficit is defined as the loss of monetary gold plus an increase in U.S. liquid liabilities to foreigners. This is in contrast to what is now called the "net liquidity balance," which includes, in addition, changes in U.S. liquid *assets* abroad. The old liquidity balance is now called "gross liquidity."

[4] A budget deficit without supporting monetary expansion would not be inflationary.

goods and services and the current balance tell pretty much the same story.

Of course, we cannot gauge a country's balance-of-payments position by the trade or the current balance alone. But on the plausible assumption that the United States, in view of its great wealth, is a "natural" net capital exporter, a current account deficit implies a disequilibrium in the balance of payments.[5]

We do not know precisely the magnitude of U.S. net "natural" capital exports, but it must be quite substantial. Direct investment clearly falls into that category. But the concept surely is not coextensive with long-term capital exports. These are often swelled by purely speculative movements and by capital flows induced by contracyclical movements in this country and abroad.[6]

In the last quarter of 1967 the dollar came under strong speculative pressure. Sterling was devalued in November, which cast doubts on the dollar. The trade and current account balances were not negative, but the surplus was small and clearly insufficient to cover normal capital exports. The deficit in the so-called basic balance shot up to $7.3 billion (annual rate), the net liquidity deficit was at the same level, the official settlement deficit was $4.2 billion, and the gold stock fell by $1 billion in one quarter.

This was an alarming deterioration. It prompted President Johnson to announce, in a dramatic New Year's Day speech (January 1, 1968), a sweeping new "program of action to eliminate the external deficit." These proposals, had they been accepted by the Congress, would have amounted to almost full-fledged exchange control. They included a heavy tax on "nonessential" foreign travel

---

[5] A trade deficit does not imply a current account deficit. It could be offset by a surplus on services. For the United States, the largest positive service item is investment income, which has been rising steadily and reached the level of $8 billion net in 1971. But since other services (including tourist expenditures) are negative and since there are remittances and military expenditures abroad to be covered, investment income though large cannot turn a sizable trade deficit into a current account surplus. No quarter showing a trade deficit has registered a current account surplus. It is therefore legitimate to regard a trade deficit for the U.S. as a sign of disequilibrium. This could change in the future if investment income continues to grow. However, this growth has been stopped by interest payments on the huge liquid liabilities (dollar balances held by foreign central banks) that have piled up in recent years.

[6] Balance-of-payments analyses often identify long-term capital flow with normal or natural movements and changes in short-term flows with speculation and cyclical fluctuations. The correspondence is, however, far from perfect. What is now called the "basic" balance, that is, current account plus long-term capital, is often not basic in any real sense but also reflects speculation and other short-term fluctuations. One example is the sudden rise in the basic deficit in late 1967 mentioned in the text below. It would be easy to cite other examples.

outside the Western Hemisphere (15 percent on tourist expenditures between $8 and $15 a day and 30 percent on expenditures exceeding $15 a day!), plus a border tax on imports and a tax refund on exports to offset the burden of domestic indirect taxes.[7] These two proposals were rejected by Congress. But mandatory restrictions on direct investment abroad and mandatory repatriation of foreign earnings, as well as a tightening of "voluntary" restraints on foreign lending by American banks and of a number of petty restrictions, were immediately put into effect by presidential executive order.[8]

Speculation, largely in the form of gold hoarding abroad, continued. This led in March 1968 to the closing of the "gold pool," a cooperative arrangement by which the major central banks, with the U.S. carrying more than half of the burden, sold gold in the London market to keep the gold price from rising. But in the first quarter of 1968, before the "two-tier" gold price system was established, the United States had lost $2 billion in gold. Later in 1968 and in 1969 there occurred an unexpected improvement: capital flows turned around sharply, the official settlement balance improved, and liquid liabilities to foreign official agencies declined despite the fact that the trade and current account balances were very weak. What happened was that capital was attracted to the United States by high interest rates and a booming stock market. At the same time the European sense of security was being shaken by the student-worker revolt in France—which caused a wage explosion, eventually led to the departure of de Gaulle, turned the French franc from one of the strongest currencies into a weak one, and forced its devaluation in August 1969. The invasion of Czechoslovakia in summer of 1968 heightened the feeling of insecurity in Europe and, by contrast, revived confidence in the dollar. But it was clearly an unnatural and unsustainable phenomenon for the richest country in the world to import capital on a large scale.

In 1970 capital flows reversed themselves once more and there was again a large deficit in the official settlement balance—although the trade balance showed a small improvement, due probably to the mild American recession that had started in November 1969 and lasted for one year. As mentioned earlier, the trade balance deteriorated sharply in the second quarter of 1971 and the deficit in the

---

[7] Details and a critical analysis of this amazing program can be found in Gottfried Haberler and Thomas D. Willett, *U.S. Balance of Payments Policies and Internal Monetary Reform: A Critical Analysis* (Washington, D. C.: American Enterprise Institute for Public Policy Research, 1968), p. 19, et seq.

[8] This was done "by virtue of the authority vested in the President by the act of October 6, 1917 as amended (12 U.S.C. 95a)."

official settlements balance jumped from $9.8 billion in 1970 to $29.8 billion in 1971, reflecting a large increase in U.S. liquid liabilities to foreign central banks which had to buy dollars to keep their currencies from rising above parity. On May 9, 1971, the German mark was allowed to float up and, following the mark, the Swiss franc and the Austrian schilling were appreciated by 7 percent and 5 percent, respectively. Austria and Switzerland had learned from their experiences in 1969 and 1970 that they exposed themselves to strong inflationary impulses ("imported inflation") from Germany, their most important trading partner, if they did not follow the mark.

Recent Developments: August 15, 1971 to June 1973

The New Economic Policy brought two important changes in the international area, suspension of gold convertibility of the dollar and a general surcharge of 10 percent on dutiable imports (equivalent to 4.8 percent surcharge on all imports).

De facto, the dollar had been inconvertible into gold for some time, in the sense that large foreign dollar holders such as the German and Japanese central banks knew that the gold window would be closed if they tried to convert some of their dollars into gold. Earlier in 1971, however, there had been some small gold conversions of dollars held by smaller countries. Since August 15, 1971, the dollar has not been convertible for anybody. This meant that, until general floating started in March 1973, the world was formally on the dollar standard rather than on the dollar-gold exchange standard.

However, two facts should be kept in mind. First the declaration of inconvertibility only legalized an existing situation. Dr. Edwin Stopper, president of the Swiss National Bank, put it this way: "According to a widely held view on 15 August 1971 the dollar-gold exchange standard was put to rest. Actually it was not the existing monetary system that broke down, but the notion that it was based on the dollar-gold exchange standard. In reality it functioned, practically from the beginning, as a dollar standard." [9]

Second, while the dollar has been inconvertible into gold for a long time (with the small exception noted above), it has remained fully convertible in the market all along. In other words, holders of dollars, foreigners as well as Americans, can use their dollars as they please to buy or invest or disinvest in the United States and can

---

[9] Address to the annual general meeting of the Swiss National Bank on 28 April 1972 (mimeographed).

exchange their dollars in the market for other currencies either at a fixed rate if the foreign currency is pegged to the dollar or at the prevailing market rate if the foreign currency floats. (For Americans the market convertibility of the dollar is somewhat restricted by the various capital export restrictions.)

It stands to reason that market convertibility of the most important currency, the dollar, is of the utmost importance to world trade. The fact that world trade has continued to grow by leaps and bounds despite frequent currency crises is to a large extent due to the fact that the dollar, and most other major currencies as well, have remained convertible in the market.[10] This is in sharp contrast to what happened during the 1930s.

The import surcharge of 10 percent was a temporary measure designed to bring pressure on surplus countries to appreciate their currencies. In that it was successful and it was promptly removed after it had served its purpose. The surcharge helped to induce the Japanese to let the yen rise. It also helped to bring about the Smithsonian agreement, which was reached on December 18, 1971, after intensive negotiations and numerous conferences at the highest level. This agreement brought a drastic realignment of exchange rates, including a depreciation of the dollar in terms of gold of 7.6 percent, a sharp appreciation of the mark, yen and Swiss franc, and a smaller one for several other currencies including sterling and the French franc.

The turmoil in the exchange market subsided, but the calm did not last long. The British balance of payments deteriorated again and, on June 23, 1972, the government was forced to let sterling float—the first post-Smithsonian crisis. The appreciation of sterling vis-à-vis the dollar in the Smithsonian Agreement thus proved to have been a mistake which probably had been made for political reasons.

The devaluation of sterling stimulated speculation against the dollar. Between July 1 and September 1, the Federal Reserve intervened in the market to support the dollar by selling a few million German marks and Belgian francs, a trifling sum of $31.5 million. This move was played up in official statements and in the press as a historic change in policy. It was merely a gesture of goodwill, one that was well received abroad and that may have eased the situation momentarily as was widely claimed by making foreign central banks more willing to buy dollars. But it could not restore confidence of

---

[10] However very few currencies are as completely convertible in the market as the dollar.

the market because the American trade deficit remained throughout the year at the record level of over $6 billion (annual rate) that it had reached in the first quarter.

The second post-Smithsonian currency crisis was touched off by European developments. The Italian lira had been weak for some time, because of unsettled internal political and economic conditions that have produced continuous uncontrollable flight of capital. On January 22, 1973, the authorities decided to follow the French example and to split the exchange market into a pegged one for current transactions and an unpegged one for capital transactions. The Italian crisis was an alarm signal. The flow of speculative funds—dollars—into Switzerland and Germany rose immediately. But the Swiss had learned their lesson. When they saw the avalanche coming, they let the franc float up (January 23, 1973) and the flood of dollars poured into Germany and Japan. Both countries at first categorically refused to either appreciate or float. So in one week (February 1 to 9) the Bundesbank had to buy over $6 billion to prevent the mark from going through the roof. Then the exchange markets were closed and the United States had to take things in hand. By offering a 10 percent devaluation of the dollar in terms of gold and SDRs, it took Germany and Japan off the hook. Japan agreed to float the yen (February 14),[11] and Germany accepted the 11.1 percent appreciation of the mark vis-à-vis the dollar (and many other currencies) that the depreciation of the dollar implied. Germany's common market partners—minus Italy and Great Britain, who continued their independent floats—went along with the mark, and a number of other countries appreciated their currencies vis-à-vis the dollar by varying smaller amounts.

But when the markets were reopened on February 14, it soon became clear that the new pattern of exchange rates had not restored confidence. Speculation continued and on March 1 the Bundesbank had to buy $2.7 billion—the largest daily flow of hot money ever recorded—to prevent the mark from rising above the new intervention point.

On March 2 the exchange markets were again closed and they remained closed officially until March 19. However unlike the earlier cases, "closing of the markets" this time merely meant that there was no official pegging. The central banks stayed out of the market, but private trading was allowed to continue and exchange rates were

---

[11] From that day on, the Italian lira, too, was allowed to float. But Italy kept its dual exchange rate—so it had a double float, one for current transactions, the other for financial transactions.

quoted. Speculation practically stopped as soon as the central banks stopped offering the speculators a one-way option by pegging, and exchange rates changed only slightly.

During the breathing spell of the float, the members of the Common Market—minus Great Britain and Italy whose currencies continue to float independently—agreed on a common float of their currencies against the dollar, after Germany had agreed to appreciate the mark by 3 percent vis-à-vis its Common Market partners and also de facto vis-à-vis the dollar and other currencies (although it has not declared a legal par value).

Since March 19 when the markets were officially reopened, the situation has been this: Yen, lira, sterling, Swiss francs and Canadian dollars float independently. The currencies of the Common Market countries—France, Germany, the Benelux countries and Denmark—plus Norway and Sweden have a "common float" against the outside. In other words, these countries link their currencies together by intervention with a 2½ percent band (maximum spread between the strongest and the weakest currency), the so-called "snake," but refrain from fixing the rate of the dollar. Thus, no attempt is made to keep the "snake" inside a "tunnel."

Actually the snake remained inside the old tunnel until early May. At that time speculation once more turned against the dollar and drove the gold price to record highs. Under the old system this would have produced a first-rate crisis and foreign central banks would have had to buy billions of dollars to keep their currencies from rising. Under the floating system some of the strong currencies, such as the mark and the Swiss franc, rose by roughly 8 percent vis-à-vis the dollar and many other currencies. Instead of ministers of finance and governors of central banks rushing around from one emergency meeting to the other, the market took care of the problem with comparatively mild fluctuations.

It is beyond the scope of this paper to describe the working of this system in detail. I confine myself to two remarks: First the various floats are by no means entirely "unmanaged." Undoubtedly the interventions have been, and still are, numerous, although it is impossible for an outsider to estimate their frequency and size.[12] Second, for almost two months after March 19 a remarkable tran-

---

[12] Even the Canadian float has been a managed one since 1970, judging from the fact that the Canadian international reserve has grown substantially during that period. This is in contrast to Canada's earlier period of floating (1950-1962) when the authorities claimed that their interventions were confined to ironing out short-run fluctuations.

quillity reigned in the exchange markets.[13] When speculation against the dollar started again in May—probably largely because of the unsettled political situation and resurgence of inflation in the United States, but also because Germany took strong anti-inflationary measures that made an appreciation of the mark a distinct possibility [14]— the market took care of the problem with mild fluctuation of exchange rates.

How long the calm will last depends primarily on how long the authorities will leave exchange markets alone and refrain from pegging. An uncertain question is how long it will be possible to keep the Common Market currencies together in a common float. That will depend on whether the members of the block will be able to coordinate their monetary, fiscal, and wage policies sufficiently. If past experience in the Common Market and elsewhere is a guide, the changes are dim that the common float will last very long.[15]

The Nature of the Recent Crisis

The currency crisis of February-March 1973 is usually called a crisis of the dollar—and so it undoubtedly was. But it was also a mark and a yen crisis. I would speak of a pure dollar crisis if the dollar were overvalued with respect to all or most currencies so that a devaluation of the dollar was all that were needed to restore equilibrium. A pure mark and yen crisis would exist if these two currencies were undervalued with respect to all or most currencies so

---

[13] At that time several people suggested that the quiet in the exchange market should be attributed not to floating but rather to the restrictions on capital inflows that had recently been put in place, especially in Germany.

This explanation is unconvincing. Twice, once in 1969 and once in 1971, Germany had gone through the exercise of first resisting appreciation and then retreating into a temporary float. In both cases, speculation ceased immediately after the authorities stopped giving the speculators a one-way option by pegging, despite the absence of elaborate capital import restrictions. On all three occasions the Bundesbank lost billions of marks by buying billions of dollars in the vain attempt to keep the mark down (not counting, as unavoidable, the loss on previously accumulated dollars).

One more example: The Swiss had elaborate capital import controls in place in 1973, but still had to resort to floating to stop speculation.

[14] Some highly respected German economic research institutions expressed doubts that the anti-inflationary policy could succeed without "protection from imported inflation" ("Aussenwirtschaftliche Absicherung" is the German expression) through a rise of the mark in the exchange market. Actually in May the mark was still at the bottom of the snake.

[15] In June Germany was, in fact, forced to appreciate the mark once more by 5.5 percent. See Postscript: Developments Since Completion of This Paper, page 99 below.

that their up-valuation was all that were needed to restore equilibrium. The recent crisis clearly was a mixture. The dollar was devalued with respect to many but by no means all currencies, and the mark and yen were up-valued with respect to many currencies but not all.

It should be observed, however, that even in a pure mark and yen crisis, the dollar would be prominently involved. Whenever one or two important currencies get out of line and seem ripe for up-valuation, dollars from all over the world, not only from the United States, will flow into these currencies. This flow will give the impression of a dollar crisis, even if the dollar is not out of line vis-à-vis any currency other than the two or even if the U.S. balance of payments is in equilibrium. This is the consequence of the fact that the dollar still is the world's foremost reserve, official intervention and private transactions currency.

It is useful to carry this thought one step further. Suppose SDRs or gold replaced the dollar as the international reserve and official intervention currency. Suppose further that one or two important currencies became undervalued. The consequences would be much the same as now—gold, SDRs and dollars would rush into the undervalued currencies. I say "and dollars" because, even if the dollar were shorn of its official reserve and intervention functions, it would still be an important private transactions currency and the American economy would still be the leading economy in the world.

This confirms the now widely accepted view that the basic defect of the present monetary system is the malfunctioning of the balance-of-payments adjustment mechanism, the "adjustable peg" system. What is needed most is greater flexibility of adjustment. It is possible that sufficient flexibility has already been achieved by widespread floating, however "dirty" or intensively managed it may be.[16] I doubt that a grand revision of the International Monetary Fund charter is

---

[16] I personally would distinguish between "dirty" floating and "managed" floating. If management is confined to buying and selling of foreign exchange in a free market for the purpose of ironing out short-run fluctuations, it does not deserve to be called "dirty." I would go further and say that even if the purpose of buying and selling is somewhat more ambitious, namely, to restrain a rapid rise or decline of the exchange rate that seems to be unjustified—in other words, if the purpose of management is to moderate an emerging trend without trying to suppress it altogether—this policy will not upset the smooth working of the system in the same way as rigid pegging does. Floating becomes "dirty" when markets are split, when special rates for different types of transactions are established in either an open or disguised form and other controls are used to influence the rates. The borderline between merely managed and "dirty" floating is fluid, but experience seems to show that the system can stand a good deal of management without developing the defects of the adjustable peg.

at all feasible or desirable. But this problem will not be further pursued in the present paper.

To say that smoother adjustment is the most pressing problem does not mean that the management of the dollar and the American inflation are unimportant for the functioning of the international monetary system. Far from it. I now turn to an analysis of the weakened position of the dollar with special emphasis on the American inflation.

The Weakness of the Dollar and the American Inflation

The American balance of payments and the dollar have been chronically weak since the late 1950s. Is this entirely a consequence of the American inflation? Our inflation surely has had much to do with it. When there was little or no inflation from 1958 to 1964, the balance of payments greatly improved: the surplus on goods and services rose from practically zero in 1959 to $8.6 billion in 1964. There can be little doubt that the U.S. balance would again improve if inflation were brought under control, even if this were done without causing a recession.[17]

However, American inflation is emphatically not the only cause of the weak U.S. balance of payments. A factor of major importance is the rapid recovery of industrial Europe and Japan and other countries, causing American industries to lose the semi-monopolistic position they enjoyed during the first years after the war.[18] Another important factor is the numerous devaluations of most currencies against the dollar that occurred during the first twenty-five years after the war: the wholesale devaluation of currencies against the dollar in 1949, four devaluations of the French franc between 1948 and 1958 (when de Gaulle put the franc on a firm basis) and one more after de Gaulle's departure in 1969, and many others.

---

[17] It is not, however, absolutely certain because it is conceivable that some countries would want to secure a surplus by devaluation, either in order to increase their international reserve or to stimulate their economy. But in view of the high propensity to inflate everywhere, I would not expect this to happen on a large scale. Moreover, the United States should not be alarmed if it happened. At any rate, foreign complaints about the excessive accumulation of dollar balances would be less insistent if the purchasing power of the dollar remained intact.

[18] To show that this is not just hindsight, let me quote what I said in my pamphlet, *Inflation: Its Causes and Cures* (Washington, D. C.: American Enterprise Institute, 1959), revised and enlarged, 1961 and 1966. "The rapid deterioration in the U.S. trade and payments position since 1957 has to be attributed mainly to the rapid recovery of industrial Europe and Japan from war destruction and dislocation . . ." (p. 68, 1961 edition).

All this, of course, does not mean that the dollar is lost or that the American inflation is irrelevant. It means, however, that in view of the weakened competitive position of American industry, equilibrium at stable exchange rates requires a much lower inflation rate, possibly a zero or negative rate, than we have actually had.

The reference to zero or negative inflation needs careful explanation. The degree of inflation is usually measured in terms of the consumer price index (CPI). Using that definition, it is definitely not true as a general proposition that all countries with less inflation than the average will enjoy surpluses and all those with more inflation will develop deficits. As a conspicuous and very important example, take the case of Japan. Starting from 1953 as 100, the Japanese CPI almost doubled by the first quarter of 1970 (rising to 197.3) whereas the U.S. consumer price index rose by less than 50 percent (to 141.4). But Japan's wholesale price index (WPI) rose by only 14 percent (to 114.1) and its export price index (EPI) even declined by 5.2 percent (to 94.8). For the United States the figures were 125.3 for the WPI and 129.6 for the EPI.

Japan's case is extreme, but it is not the only case. Is has been found that the higher a country's productivity growth (output per man-hour), the greater is the gap between the CPI and WPI. Thus, the rapidly growing economies of Germany, Italy and Japan have displayed a significantly higher CPI/WPI ratio than the slowly growing economies of Canada, the United States and the United Kingdom.[19] The well-known reason is that the CPI is heavily weighted with services, including distribution services at each stage on a product's way to the final consumer. These services are on the whole labor-intensive and have a slower productivity growth than manufacturing industries and agriculture. With respect to the CPI/EPI ratio, the contrast between the high and low productivity countries is even greater. The explanation is partly the same as in the case of the CPI/WPI ratio. In addition, the good performance with respect to export prices of the three high-productivity countries mentioned above, Germany, Italy and Japan, surely is connected with the rapid recovery of those countries after the war. The principal rapidly

[19] See Ronald McKinnon, *Monetary Theory and Controlled Flexibility in the Foreign Exchanges*, Essays in International Finance No. 84 (Princeton, N. J.: Princeton University Press, 1971). See also Bela Balassa's important paper, "The Purchasing Power Parity Doctrine: A Reappraisal," *Journal of Political Economy*, vol. 72 (1964). A careful statistical analysis has been made by Hirotaka Kato, "Statistical Analysis of the Gap between Consumer Price and Wholesale Price Movements in Japan, 1960-1964," in *Shokei Ronso* (Kanagawa University, Japan), vol. II, no. 4 (March 1967).

growing exports of the three countries are manufactured commodities, especially durable ones. These are the industries with the most rapid recovery and productivity growth.[20]

But whatever the complete explanation, the difference between the United States and some other important countries with respect to the divergence between consumer prices on the one hand and wholesale and export prices on the other has far-reaching economic consequences. Suppose the United States succeeds in stopping inflation in the sense that consumer prices remain stable. Since the prices and price levels of internationally traded goods in different countries are closely linked and move together, the larger gap in Germany and Japan between the WPI and EPI on the one hand and the CPI on the other implies that their CPIs would have to rise substantially vis-à-vis that of the United States if equilibrium in the balance of payments is to be maintained at fixed exchange rates. In other words, there is a sort of inflation-transmission multiplier at work. Inflation in the United States whether zero or positive, is transmitted in a significantly amplified manner to some other countries in terms of the CPI.

This has important implications for the future of the international monetary system, especially for one that is based on the dollar. It has often been said that as long as the world is on the dollar standard—that is to say, as long as most countries peg their currencies to the dollar and keep them convertible—the U.S. sets the pace for world inflation. It is true that in principle the price relationship is reciprocal: U.S. inflation induces inflation in all countries that maintain fixed exchange rates and inflation abroad induces inflation in the United States. But, as an empirical propostion, the relationship is assymetrical. This follows from the fact, or what I take as a fact, that American inflation is almost entirely determined by domestic policies—domestic policy objectives and constraints—and is only marginally influenced by forces from abroad.[21] Twenty years ago monetary and fiscal policies which determine the pace of inflation

---

[20] It should be kept in mind that in the United States, and presumably elsewhere too, the EPI is statistically a much poorer and less reliable index than the CPI and WPI. In the case of Japan one could also think of lower "dumping" prices as an explanatory factor. But in view of the American sensitivity to dumping, flagrant cases of dumping are unlikely to escape detection and are subject to countervailing and anti-dumping measures.

[21] William D. Nordhaus, "The Worldwide Wage Explosion," *Brookings Papers on Economic Activity*, 2: 1972 (Washington, D. C.: The Brookings Institution, 1972), reaches a fair conclusion. "How does the U.S. exert such a powerful influence on prices abroad? Paradoxically, the answer is because the U.S. is the only country that does not (or can afford not to) care seriously about the effect of its price level on its external position." (P. 459.) Actually there is nothing paradoxical about that.

in the United States were still influenced by balance-of-payments considerations. This is no longer the case and most economists agree that it should not be the case. It is the principal postulate of the policy of benign neglect that macroeconomic policies should be determined by domestic policy objectives and not by the balance of payments. Even officials who reject the policy of benign neglect accept its basic postulate. Thus, Arthur Burns's famous Ten Commandments for international monetary reform state that the "international monetary system will have to respect the need for substantial autonomy of domestic monetary policies. . . . No country . . . should have to accept sizable increases in unemployment to reduce its deficit. Nor should a surplus country have . . . [to accept] high rates of inflation [to reduce its surplus]." [22]

The cyclical situation and the rate of inflation in the United States are, of course, subject to some influences from abroad via the balance of payments and more directly through exchange rate changes. For example, the large trade deficit of $6.8 billion in 1972 must have helped a little to dampen inflation, and the 1973 devaluation of the dollar somewhat exacerbated the inflationary trend through the rise in import prices even before it began to have a favorable effect on the balance of payments.

But for the United States these repercussions and feedbacks are normally minor and can be offset, and are likely to be offset, by domestic policy changes. For all other Western countries, however, they are of major importance.[23] Because of this quantitative assymetry, we can say that the United States sets the pace for world inflation, that is, it sets the pace for inflation in the many countries that peg their currencies to the dollar and keep them convertible.

So long as exchange rates are fixed and currencies remain convertible, this is a fact of life that would not be changed even if the dollar were replaced by SDRs. Only by changing parities or by floating can other countries stay out of the backwash of the American inflation.

To say, as I do bluntly, that the United States sets the pace of world inflation, does not mean that the United States is responsible for every inflation in the world. Many countries have managed to generate, autonomously and voluntarily, more inflation than we have.

---

[22] Arthur F. Burns, "Some Essentials of International Monetary Reform," Federal Reserve Bank of New York Monthly Review, June 1972, p. 132 (address to the 1972 International Banking Conference, Montreal, Canada, 12 May 1972).

[23] If the U.S. trade balance shifted from the current deficit of almost $7 billion to a larger surplus of $13 billion, which sometimes is mentioned as a target, it would be a highly inflationary factor.

This is clearly true of the many countries that have been forced at one time or another to devalue vis-à-vis the dollar. It is also true of some that have kept their currencies stable in terms of dollars, although in that case the fact is a little more difficult to establish. If a country has trouble keeping its external balance in equilibrium (symptoms: use of controls, loss of reserves) and is forced from time to time to depreciate, we can conclude that it is generating its inflation autonomously, although this often does not inhibit such a country from loudly complaining that the U.S. is exporting inflation.

On the other hand, if a country has more inflation measured by the CPI than the United States, it may nevertheless be argued that it has been subject to unwanted inflationary pressure from the U.S., for its more rapidly rising CPI may be due to the working of what I have called the inflation-transmission multiplier.

Some writers have tried to demonstrate that most countries that have been complaining about being forced to "import inflation" from the United States have in reality made their inflations all by themselves. The demonstration takes the form of showing that, in the crucial years, the central banks of those countries have increased their domestic assets just as much or more than their foreign assets. The idea is that we can speak of imported inflation only if the increase in the money supply is substantially equal to, and is due to, an increase in the international reserve, reflecting a favorable balance of payments, irrespective of whether the reserve flow stems from current transactions (trade surplus) or capital movements (including speculative funds).

This seems to me an unduly narrow interpretation of the matter. True, both an imported inflation (rise in prices) and a homemade one have to be supported by an increase in the quantity of money. But whether this increase comes entirely from central bank purchases of *foreign* assets (increases in their international reserves) or partly or predominately from purchases of *domestic* assets (open market operations or loans) is a matter of secondary importance. If the latter is the case, that is, if the acquisition of domestic assets is partly or largely responsible for the increase in the money supply, it may reflect a deliberate policy designed to forestall an undue accumulation of dollars or it may be the consequence of a boom touched off by heavy orders from abroad. In neither case does it preclude a perfectly honest statement to the effect that the inflation was imported, in the sense that it would not have occurred if the balance of payments had not gone into surplus. The basic fact is that prices and price levels in countries engaged in intensive trade with one another are closely

94

connected through the medium of tradable-goods prices which, allowing for transportation costs, are the same at home and abroad. Therefore such price levels react promptly to inflationary impulses from abroad and to changes in exchange rates.[24] Whether a given country follows the U.S. inflation reluctantly, is seriously inconvenienced and hence can be said to be subjected to unwanted imported inflation, or whether it generates enough inflation at home to get into balance-of-payments troubles even if there were no U.S. inflation—the answer to this hypothetical question cannot be deduced solely from the ratio of foreign to domestic assets in the central bank of the country concerned. Additional evidence is required to decide this question, such as a loss of reserves, resort to controls and occasional devaluations.

This analysis should not be interpreted, however, as a denial or disregard of the fact that no country need submit to imported inflation. On the contrary, I believe that any country can, in principle, shield itself from foreign inflation by appreciating or floating.[25] In fact, appreciation and floating are the only really effective defenses against imported inflation. Large countries with a small foreign trade sector may be able to resist inflationary pressures from abroad by using open market operations to offset the monetary expansion caused by the influx of reserves and to reduce the prices of nontraded goods as a counter to the price increases of traded goods. But there obviously are economic, political, psychological, and institutional limits to this increasingly costly policy. Small countries will reach these limits quickly. The longer a country resists, the more the inflationary pressure will be intensified by speculation. Small countries are likely to be overwhelmed in a short time.

But let me repeat, the compulsion to submit to imported inflation arises only under a regime of fixed exchanges and convertibility.[26]

---

[24] By appreciating its currency a country exerts inflationary pressure on its neighbors who refuse to go along. For example the German appreciation in 1969 had a strong inflationary impact on Austria and Switzerland. These countries learned their lesson and followed Germany immediately in its next appreciation in 1971. In 1973 Switzerland floated before Germany moved.

By parity of reason, it follows that by depreciating its currency a country exerts *anti-inflationary* pressure on its neighbors who refuse to go along. This is, of course, true only if currencies are convertible in the market.

[25] It should not be overlooked, however, that monetary influences from abroad—inflationary and especially deflationary influences—often have an admixture of *real* shifts in international demand. These real shifts cannot be obviated by monetary measures such as parity changes.

[26] It is well known that inconvertibility, that is, propping up a nominally fixed exchange rate by a battery of controls, is analytically (not merely definitionally) equivalent to disguised devaluation or upvaluation with multiple exchange rates.

Some Implications for the Future of the International Monetary System

The fact that the U.S. inflation rate, whether positive or zero, is amplified as it is transmitted to some other countries makes the operations of the fixed-rate system more difficult. For this means that even if the United States managed to keep its rate of inflation at an internally tolerable and sustainable level of not more than, say, a 2 percent annual rise in the CPI, it may involve what may be an unacceptable rise of, say, 4 percent in some other countries such as Germany and Japan. In other words, because of this multiplication factor, the United States is capable of "exporting inflation" even if it has none internally.[27] This clearly strengthens the case for flexible exchange rates. The problem is, of course, greatly aggravated when the United States has rates of inflation of 4 or 5 percent because then many currencies, not just a few, become undervalued vis-à-vis the dollar.

The problem would not go away if the dollar were replaced as an international reserve and official intervention currency by SDRs, for it will always be a difficult job to devalue the world's most important private transactions currency. The reluctance of surplus countries to appreciate their currencies vis-à-vis the dollar has, one gets the impression, little to do with the reserve and official intervention function of the dollar. Rather it seems primarily motivated by the fear of losing a trade surplus, a mercantilistic attitude to be sure, and the superstition that changing an exchange rate as such is a burden.[28] There is furthermore the understandable apprehension in

---

[27] In the early 1960s when there were complaints abroad that the United States "exported inflation" through its deficit, American officials replied indignantly that America had no inflation and therefore could not export it. This was little comfort to other countries which had to submit to inflationary pressures from the American deficit. But the Americans were right in the sense that it would not be reasonable in the modern world to ask for more than price stability. To avoid exporting inflation—in other words to enable some other countries to enjoy a stable CPI at fixed parities—the United States would have had to let its CPI go down. But if the United States had a slightly declining price level—which, it will be remembered, many economists used to regard as the optimal policy—it surely would be accused by some of "exporting deflation" because quite a few countries would not be able to maintain parity with a dollar that gained steadily in purchasing power.

[28] Economists have nurtured this superstition by emphasizing, for want of economic arguments, the alleged "political" and "psychological" burdens of changing parities. In France, where the mercantilistic tradition is especially strong, official spokesmen have made it abundantly clear that their reluctance to see the franc appreciate vis-à-vis the dollar is motivated by the wish to protect French industries from what they regard as excessive American competition.

surplus countries about the danger of overadjustment (overshooting the equilibrium rate). After all, the equilibrium rate is not known and nobody wants to see a surplus position turned into one of deficit. For this reason, there is an entirely rational tendency under the adjustable peg system to appreciate too little rather than too much. If this appraisal is approximately correct, putting SDRs in the place of the dollar would achieve very little.[29]

The upshot is that, in the future, we have to expect the emergence from time to time of disequilibria which require parity changes. The dollar will probably be involved even if the United States manages to curb inflation. But with a U.S. inflation, the problem becomes much more serious.

Under the adjustable peg, parity changes are bound to be preceded and accompanied by currency crises triggered by increasingly massive flows of speculative funds. Controls on speculative capital flows is not the answer. The longer they last and the more often they are applied, the less effective they become unless they are progressively tightened. They hit "legitimate" or "virtuous" capital along with "speculative" or "bad" capital and sooner or later require current account controls as well. This cannot be further discussed here. I confine myself to drawing attention to a neglected aspect that has become very important in the last crisis: When speculative capital flows are increasingly subjected to controls, speculation turns more and more to commodities. When it becomes difficult and expensive to speculate in marks and yens, the next best thing is to get out of currencies expected to depreciate by making speculative purchases of international traded commodities.[30] This seems to have happened on a very large scale during the last crisis and to have greatly contributed to the sharp rise in raw material prices.[31] This development is a natural extension of the familiar phenomenon of "leads and lags." Gold speculation is another manifestation of the same phenomenon. But, fortunately, the price of gold does not enter the cost-of-living

---

[29] To replace the dollar as a "pivot" or "numéraire" in which parities are expressed has already been achieved to some extent because numerous new par values or central rates including that of the dollar have been officially declared in terms of SDRs. It is, however, a change of negligible importance except on the question-begging assumption that it will make parity changes, including that of the dollar, easier.

[30] "Speculation" should be interpreted in a broad sense. It means not only speculation in commodities by people who are not engaged in production or in exporting and importing of the commodities concerned—"pure speculators" we may call them—but also, and primarily, speculative purchases and orders by producing firms (national and multinational corporations) and by professional exporters and importers.

[31] See an illuminating article in *The Economist* (April 14-20, 1973).

index or the wholesale price index. Given the current huge volume of world trade, leads and lags, forward buying, and commodity speculation can move many billions of dollars from country to country in a short time. To restrict this sort of speculative flow would require tight controls going far beyond the financial area.

The conclusion is that floating is the only way to effect parity changes without setting in motion increasingly massive and disruptive capital flows. This is now being widely recognized in official circles.[32] How much floating is required remains to be seen. Rapidly accumulating experience suggests that even extensively managed floating creates enough uncertainty about the future movements of exchange rates to discourage most speculators. The German periods of floating (1969, 1971 and 1973), the Canadian case and the Brazilian "trotting peg" all point in that direction.[33]

Let me end with a cautionary note. If the American inflation is not stopped and if the dollar becomes overvalued from time to time vis-à-vis numerous currencies, there will be plenty of trouble in the international field. This trouble can be greatly reduced by floating of the currencies concerned, but it cannot be completely eliminated. Repeated devaluations of the dollar are bound to make more acute attempts on the part of official dollar holders to diversify their reserves by shifting some of their dollars into other currencies. This dangerous development, which seems to have started already, cannot be dealt with by floating.[34] But this is not an argument for the adjustable peg. On the contrary, because it breeds more and more crises, the adjustable peg system is apt to heighten the danger of instability by causing shifts of the ballast of official reserves in the hold of the international monetary ship.

[32] The German Bundesbank in its annual report for 1972, after a careful examination of what capital controls can and cannot do, reaches this conclusion: "The main lesson of past experience is that in case of confidence crises involving the dollar, in view of the large dollar balances which can be shifted around, the only effective defense against unwanted inflows is temporary setting free of the dollar exchange rate"—that is, temporary floating.

[33] On the Brazilian experience, see Juergen B. Donges, *Brazil's Trotting Peg: A New Approach to Greater Exchange Rate Flexibility in Less Developed Countries*, with an introduction by Gottfried Haberler which discusses the lessons of the Brazilian experiment for the industrial countries (Washington, D. C.: American Enterprise Institute, 1971). On the Canadian case, see Paul Wonnacott *The Floating Canadian Dollar: Exchange Flexibility and Monetary Independence* (Washington, D. C.: American Enterprise Institute, 1972).

[34] It can, of course, be argued that the adoption of a general system of freely floating parities would not require large official reserves and would therefore automatically eliminate the danger in question. But such a radical reform surely is most unlikely to materialize and, even if it did, the problems of official reserves would remain during a long period of transition.

It would go beyond the scope of an essay devoted to analyzing the international implications of the American inflation to discuss the proposals that have been made to cope with the danger of official reserve shifts.[35] If inflation were curbed in America, the danger of shifts of dollar reserves would be dramatically reduced if not entirely eliminated.

Ceterum censeo inflationem esse delendam.[36]

Postscript: Developments since Completion of This Paper*

Since this paper was completed (late May 1973) exchange markets have remained troubled and confidence in the dollar has not been restored. The exchange value of the dollar against some major currencies has sharply dropped—especially the German mark and the Swiss franc. On June 29 the mark had to be appreciated again vis-à-vis the other currencies in the common float, this time by 5.5 percent, to prevent it from piercing the back of the "snake" and so demolishing the common float. The Swiss franc continued its independent float, but substantially followed the course of the mark. On July 2 the Austrian schilling was appreciated by 4.8 percent to neutralize the inflationary backwash of the German appreciation. The pound, the lira and the Canadian dollar continued their floats but stayed more or less with the dollar. From June 4 to July 6 the mark rose vis-à-vis the dollar by 15.41 percent, the Swiss franc by 12.62 percent, and the French franc by 10.28 percent.[37]

It should be noted that these figures, which have been widely publicized, give a greatly exaggerated impression of the depreciation of the dollar since the beginning of the float or since May. Actually the value of the dollar has not much changed since March vis-à-vis the great majority of currencies. It has not declined in recent months against the currencies of countries with which the United States does about three-quarters of its trade. Among these currencies are not only

---

[35] Let me mention, however, a proposal by Professor William Fellner that would be helpful in this connection. He recommended that the U.S. consider offering to official holders of dollar balances abroad "low interest securities carrying a purchasing-power guarantee." (William Fellner, "The Dollar's Place in the International System," *The Journal of Economic Literature*, American Economic Association, vol. X, no. 3 (September 1972); available also from American Enterprise Institute, Washington, D. C., AEI Reprint No. 8.)

[36] "For the rest, I hold that inflation ought to be destroyed." Paraphrased from Marcus Porcius Cato, The Censor.

* Written July 15, 1973.

[37] The figures represent averages of buying and selling rates at noon in New York.

sterling, the lira, the Canadian dollar and many others of lesser importance, but also the yen.[38] Until July 13 the overall trade-weighted depreciation of the dollar against twenty-one OECD countries has been 3.7 percent from March 30 and 4 percent from May 4, 1973. What has happened since May is best described as a sharp appreciation, vis-à-vis the dollar and most other currencies, of the mark, the Swiss franc and the Austrian schilling to a lesser extent of the other currencies in the common float.

The lack of confidence in the dollar is not difficult to explain in general terms.[39] After two formal devaluations, the dollar's stability is no longer taken for granted. This has induced many foreign dollar holders, private ones as well as some official institutions, to diversify their currency holdings by shifting part of their dollars into other currencies, especially the mark. It also has alerted many people to the need to watch for symptoms of weakness in the dollar. The resurgence of inflation in the United States and the debilitating effect of the Watergate affair on the administration's ability to pursue a consistently vigorous anti-inflation policy and to resist spending pressures from Congress and special interests surely were two of the major factors sparking the new wave of speculation. Others were Germany's very energetic anti-inflation measures and the strong showing of its balance of payments, which made the mark an obvious candidate for appreciation. Because of the common float arrangement the mark pulls up other currencies.[40] As explained above, any such speculation is bound to focus particularly on the dollar.

---

[38] There has been a sharp contrast between the yen and the mark. While the mark has sharply appreciated, the yen-dollar rate has changed little since March. Space does not permit an analysis of this remarkable development. But it may be mentioned that the Bank of Japan has been able to reduce its dollar holdings by about $4 billion. Without these interventions the yen would have depreciated somewhat and the dollar would be correspondingly higher. The Japanese current account surplus has for the time being disappeared. Japan seems to have been importing raw materials on a grand scale.

[39] This is true only ex post. I do not claim that I have foreseen the recent appreciation of the mark and other currencies or any of the specific crises mentioned earlier in this paper. I could easily give documentary evidence for this statement, but I could also prove that the same is true of the vast majority of economists, official as well as academic, working in the field of international finance. It is one thing to demonstrate that the system of the adjustable peg is crisis-prone, and an entirely different thing to forecast with any accuracy the timing and intensity of particular crises or waves of speculation.

[40] Thus once again the disruptive power of fixed exchange rates in the absence of a sufficient coordination of policies has been strikingly demonstrated. Before appreciating the mark on June 29 the Bundesbank had to buy DM 4 billions' worth of the other currencies in the common float in a futile attempt to keep

It is true that, measured in terms of the consumer price index, the American inflation has been substantially less than the inflations in Germany, Switzerland, Japan and elsewhere. But the German export boom has not yet faltered and the market has learned that differential rates of inflation are not always, at least not in the short and medium run, a good guide for exchange rate developments. (The reasons are analyzed above, pages 91-92.)

Sophisticated observers and speculators are perturbed by the failure of U.S. monetary authorities to control the money supply. In 1972 the rate of monetary growth was at its highest level since the Korean War, 8.9 percent. True, it was down 2.2 percent during the first quarter of 1973, but it shot up to 10.3 percent during the second (annual rates). The attempt to substitute suppression of symptoms of inflation for resolute elimination of inflation's causes, to freeze and control prices instead of putting a firm rein on monetary growth and raising taxes, does not inspire confidence. The unanimous support of the Democratic caucus in the Senate for a "90-day freeze on prices, profits, rents, wages and salaries, and consumer interest rates"—many even asked for a rollback of prices—and the inability of an embattled administration to stand up to such irrational and hysterical demands has made a deplorable impression.[11] So has the haphazard imposition of restrictions on the export of important commodities.

It will be recalled that in 1971 one of the main justifications for controls was that "excess demand had been eliminated from the system"—presumably by monetary restraints. The remaining inflation, it was said, was due to cost-push pressures and inflationary psychology, for which wage and price controls were the only cure. It was difficult to attach a precise meaning to the phrase "excess demand has been eliminated," for neither the quantity of money (M) nor total expenditure (nominal income, MV) had stopped growing.[42] But what-

---

the mark in the snake. True to form the German minister of finance vehemently denied any intention to appreciate only a few hours before the decision to do so was announced. He went out of his way to attack the "irresponsible professors" at the Institute in Kiel. Their transgression had been to warn that the German anti-inflation policy could not succeed and would lose its credibility without protection against inflationary influences from abroad.

[41] An overwhelming majority of the Democratic senators also voted for a large increase in the minimum wage—which is, in effect, a vote for more inflation and more unemployment, especially of underprivileged workers (such as teenagers and blacks).

[42] What had been squeezed, though of course not eliminated, was profits. It would have made more sense to use the Keynesian phrase that inflation was no longer a "profit inflation," but an "income inflation" (cost inflation).

ever the advocates of controls originally had in mind, there seems to be general agreement that wage-push has not been the moving force in 1973. The new inflation is a demand inflation. Therefore the original justification for controls is no longer applicable.[43] The new price freeze was imposed at a most inopportune time and it caused most serious wastes and distortions almost immediately.

It almost looks as if the administration had wanted to demonstrate the absurdity of a price freeze. In that it may have succeeded. The majority of the senators who had demanded a general freeze voted a few weeks later, when beef became scarce, to abolish the freeze on beef prices. Moreover there is some evidence that the debacle of the American price freeze and control of 1973 served as a warning example to some foreign countries such as Germany which have not yet tried it themselves. (The 1971 freeze and Phase II may have had the opposite effect, because it was oversold as a great success, although in retrospect few would continue to make the exaggerated claims that were made earlier.)

The disillusionment with controls is a very healthy development. But there is danger that it may go too far in one respect: Wage pressure by labor unions will again become the most serious stumbling block to regaining price stability. Much praise has been heaped on unions for their moderation. But workers' earnings are rising at an annual rate of 7 percent. This may be moderate under present inflation. But will unions accept a slower wage growth of, say, 3 to 4 percent—which is probably the maximum compatible with price stability? I doubt it. I am afraid that we shall soon be confronted again with the problem of wage push by monopolistic unions. Monopolies require controls. The tragedy was that price controls were applied indiscriminately to a largely competitive economy. The debacle of this policy should not be allowed to compromise monopoly control. And labor unions are the most powerful monopolists.

The 1973 surge in prices has made the international character of inflation more conspicuous than it was formerly. Monetary authorities in most countries have seized the opportunity to plead innocence and to blame inflation on other countries and on anonymous international markets. Small and medium sized countries are indeed, as we have seen, powerless to avoid world price trends unless they are

---

[43] It is sometimes said that we still have a case of cost-inflation because the sharp rise in raw material prices has raised production costs. But this makes little sense, since most raw materials, feedstuffs and foodstuffs are traded in highly competitive international markets. If the worldwide surge in demand for raw materials is not a case of demand inflation, it is difficult to see what would be one.

ready to float. (And even floating does not ensure immediate success.) But for very large countries such as the United States, the scope for blaming others is very limited. Without the excessive monetary expansion and large government deficit in 1972, the domestic component of the U.S. inflation would have been at least much smaller than it was, and the imported component, would also have been smaller because it is partly the result of inflation previously exported from the United States.

As mentioned earlier a shift of foreign official dollar holdings into German marks and possibly other currencies has been underway. The German Bundesbank stated in its last annual report that the mark has become the second largest reserve currency (but did not divulge the names of the countries involved). This type of portfolio readjustment by official dollar holders may put pressure on the dollar for a considerable period, unless U.S. inflation is credibly curbed or an international agreement on official reserve holdings is reached. Readjustment of private currency holdings on the other hand can be assumed to run its course quickly.

Given these adverse factors, the present system of widespread floating surely has worked much better than the former system of the adjustable peg would have. It is not hard to visualize what would have happened under the earlier arrangements: huge flows of dollars into Germany, Switzerland, Japan, and so forth; ministers of finance and presidents of central banks rushing around from one emergency meeting to another; a rash of controls on the international movement of funds and eventually devaluations, upvaluations—and floats.

This is not to say, however, that the present situation is satisfactory. In particular there is almost general agreement—this time shared not only by officials, who have to profess optimism, but also by the great majority of independent experts—that the dollar is now undervalued in the sense that, at current exchange rates, the United States is likely to develop after some delay a large export surplus. In other words, it is widely believed that speculation against the dollar has gone too far and that the current pessimism about the dollar's future is excessive.

It is argued in the body of this paper that occasional judicious management of a float by intervention in the exchange market need not deprive the float of its beneficial effect or signify a return to the crisis-prone system of the adjustable peg, so long as such management stops short of rigid pegging at a specific rate. I have argued elsewhere at greater length that situations may arise, especially when noneconomic, political factors are involved, where the speculators and the markets are wrong.[44] In such cases government intervention in the market—that is, counter-speculation—is in order.

There is reason to believe that we have such a situation today, in which case the dollar should be supported by official intervention in the market. From a technical standpoint it does not matter who intervenes, the United States selling gold and foreign exchange for dollars, or foreign central banks buying dollars. But since psychology and politics are heavily involved it is very important that intervention, if it takes place, be done with international agreement. These highly important tactical problems can be discussed here only briefly.

As far as the U.S. is concerned, it should use its gold stock which is quite large at the current free market price, to bring down the price of gold and support the dollar.[45] The alternative—or supplement —to gold sales would be to borrow marks and other currencies from the International Monetary Fund (IMF) or from foreign central banks. This course has been strongly urged by the Europeans. From the standpoint of impact on the exchange market, it comes to the same whether Germany buys dollars with marks or the United States borrows the marks to buy dollars. Moreover, both alternatives would cause the German money supply to expand, a consequence that would tend to counteract the anti-inflation policy of the Bundesbank. The economic difference, however, is that by borrowing foreign currencies abroad the United States in effect would give an exchange guarantee to the foreign central bank.[46] But if we are sure that the dollar is undervalued and is likely to rise after the wave of adverse speculation has been broken or reversed, the exchange risk should be no serious deterrent.

---

[44] See "The Case Against Capital Controls for Balance of Payments Reasons," a paper prepared for the Geneva Conference on *Capital Movements and Their Control*, June 15-16, 1973 (to be published). It is argued there that these are exceptional cases and that it is much easier to think of cases where the speculators' judgment about the strength or weakness of a currency was right and that of the authorities wrong than of cases where the opposite was true. But we cannot exclude the possibility of waves of excessive optimism or pessimism concerning the true value of a currency.

[45] It has been suggested that the U.S. should sell large amounts of its gold in the free market even if no international agreement on such sales could be reached. This would, however, not be advisable for, as Professor Fellner has pointed out to me, this policy would run the risk that some foreign central banks might seize the opportunity to get rid of some of their dollars. In that case selling gold would mean throwing gold into a bottomless pit.

[46] In case of borrowing from the IMF even a gold guarantee would be involved according to the Articles of Agreement. This is another instance where recent events have made the Articles of Agreement obsolete.

One last word: it should be clear that even massive interventions would do no good in the absence of a firm anti-inflation policy that does not tinker with symptoms by imposing haphazard controls on prices and exports but goes to the root of the trouble by putting a tight rein on money supply and doing something decisive about the budget by reducing expenditures or raising taxes.

After the last meeting of the Committee of Twenty of the International Monetary Fund, the ministers of finance expressed great optimism that agreement on reforming the international monetary system could be reached early next year and the reform be put into effect a year later. Details have not yet been divulged but several ministers have stated that the new system will again be based on semi-fixed parities; exchange rates will be "stable but adjustable," as the disingenuous phrase goes.

Before abandoning floating, the ministers would be well advised to do their homework and curb inflation. The reason behind this advice is that fixed or semi-fixed exchange rates require close coordination of monetary, fiscal and wage policies—or, expressed differently, mutually consistent rates of inflation. (In other words, not "equal" rates but "consistent" rates, meaning a little more inflation for some countries, a little less for others, according to circumstances.) It is conceivable, although by no means easy or certain, that the major countries may achieve such a mutually consistent pattern, if the rates of inflation are very low everywhere. For in that case no country would find itself saddled with a very high rate of inflation. But it is practically inconceivable that there can be found such a mutually acceptable and consistent pattern, except perhaps among small groups of countries, if inflation rates cluster as they do now around an 8 percent price rise or more per annum.

4

WAGE STABILIZATION POLICY AND THE NIXON ADMINISTRATION

Marten Estey

This essay approaches the wage stabilization program of the Nixon administration, from Phase I through Phase III, as an example of national economic bargaining which, in form as well as content, reflected experience gained in previous American wage stabilization programs. Controls are given some credit for the considerable slowdown in the rate of negotiated increases under both the construction and general wage stabilization programs, but it is emphasized that since the stabilization program involved institutional as well as economic goals, its success cannot be measured solely in terms of its effectiveness in reducing inflation.

Introduction

American experience with wage stabilization policies—or more specifically, with wage restraints, whether mandatory or voluntary—is neither as recent nor as limited as may be generally supposed. In fact, Phase I and Phase II represent the fourth time in thirty years (or fifth, depending on how one counts) that the United States has adopted some form of wage stabilization policy, or incomes policy, as it is now known.

Controls designed to keep wages from rising too rapidly were first used as a wartime measure. During World War II wage stabilization was administered by the National War Labor Board from October 1942 through December 1945; the task of terminating these wartime controls was assigned to the NWLB's successor, the National Wage Stabilization Board, which ran from January 1946 through

February 1947. During the Korean War, a Wage Stabilization Board was established, and it functioned with varying effectiveness from 1950 until February 1953.[1]

In 1962, voluntary wage-price guideposts were issued by President Kennedy's Council of Economic Advisers, largely as a measure to prevent an anticipated expansion from becoming inflationary; they are generally considered to have been abandoned after 1966, although the CEA continued to set forth guidepost policy up to January 1969, when President Johnson's final *Economic Report* was issued.

Thus the general wage stabilization program of the Nixon administration, which began with the ninety-day freeze announced on August 15, 1971, and as of this writing is about to enter Phase IV, has not been a venture into uncharted waters. On the contrary, many of the basic policies and mechanisms of wage stabilization, especially under Phase II, reflected lessons learned from previous wage stabilization experience.

Economic Stabilization Act of 1970. What may be considered the first step in the present stabilization program was taken in August 1970 when Congress, over the opposition of the President, passed the Economic Stabilization Act of 1970. This act gave the President the then unwanted "standby" authority to impose controls to stabilize prices, rents, wages, and salaries. But by February 1971 when the act was due to expire, the administration's position had shifted to the extent of announcing that it would "accept" its renewal for two years. Rather ironically, it was little more than a month later, on March 29, 1971, that the administration resorted to this standby authority in order to establish the Construction Industry Stabilization Committee (CISC) and mandatory controls on wages in the construction industry—the first of its wage control programs.[2]

In fact, the Economic Stabilization Act of 1970, as amended from year to year, became the basic legislation on which the whole stabilization program of the Nixon administration rested—from the

---

[1] For a history of wage stabilization during World War II and Korea, see Abraham L. Gitlow, *Wage Determination Under National Boards* (New York: Prentice-Hall, 1953). For a brief summary, see Milton Derber, "Wage Stabilization: Then and Now. The Wage Stabilization Program in Historical Perspective," *Labor Law Journal*, August 1972, pp. 453-462.

[2] For further details on the origins of the CISC, see Marten Estey, "Wages and Wage Policy, 1962-1971," in Phillip Cagan et al., *Economic Policy and Inflation in the Sixties* (Washington, D. C.: American Enterprise Institute, 1972), pp. 155-195.

Construction Industry Stabilization Committee on through Phases I, II, III, and IV.

The Decision to Adopt General Wage Controls. Although it initiated wage controls in construction in March 1971, the Nixon administration did not turn to *general* wage controls until August. A variety of factors contributed to this decision— a decision, it should be recalled, which seemed all the more surprising because it was a complete reversal of the administration's long-standing opposition to controls.

Perhaps most obvious was the rising public pressure for controls, both from business and political leaders. This, in turn, reflected the fact that the policy of economic restraint, which had been the keystone of the administration's initial effort for coping with inflation, had not only failed to produce any significant reduction in the rate of inflation, but had compounded the economic problem by provoking a rise in the unemployment rate from 3.5 percent in 1969 to 6.0 percent in the first half of 1971. Thus the seasonally adjusted unemployment rate was 5.8 percent in July, no lower than it had been six months earlier; and it was expected to rise in August because of layoffs in the steel industry (the August unemployment rate subsequently proved to be 6.1 percent). Further evidence of the extent of slack in the economy was the fact that the capacity utilization rate in manufacturing, was down to 75.4 percent in the second quarter of 1971.

After easing in the first quarter of 1971 to an annual rate of 2.4 percent, the consumer price index had turned up again in the second quarter, rising at an annual rate of 6.0 percent in June. Equally disconcerting was the 8.4 percent rise on an annual basis in wholesale industrial prices in July, the steepest increase since August 1956.

The wage picture did not offer much hope for an early reduction of cost pressures. First-year wage increases in collective bargaining settlements in manufacturing were 8.7 percent versus 8.1 percent for the full year of 1970—although in nonmanufacturing (excluding construction) there was some easing, with average increases of 11.9 percent as against 14.2 percent for the full year of 1970. And the principal measures of wage movements in the private nonfarm economy showed an acceleration in the first half of 1971; average hourly earnings rose 7.2 percent in the first six months of 1971 as against 5.3 percent for 1970, and compensation per man-hour rose 8.4 percent compared to 6.8 percent for 1970.

But as in 1962 when the Kennedy administration introduced its wage-price guidelines, the critical factor in the decision appeared to involve international rather than domestic economic policy considerations. In trying to cope with an international monetary and balance-of-payments crisis, the administration was convinced that bold action on the domestic front—in the form of the imposition of general wage and price controls—would "assure our trading partners of our intentions and provide the framework for a cooperative approach to the solution of international payments problems." [3]

The combination of circumstances in August 1971, therefore, seemed particularly well-suited to the introduction of an incomes policy. The widespread public demand for such a policy ensured its acceptance, at least initially. The country was suffering from precisely those ailments for which incomes policy is designed to give relief (though not necessarily to cure): domestic price inflation, unemployment, and balance-of-payments problems. And last, but not least, the substantial unemployment and slack in the economy provided the economic setting in which an incomes policy would be most likely to succeed.

Phase I: The Wage-Price Freeze

Accordingly, the announcement of the New Economic Policy on August 15, 1971 included a ninety-day wage-price freeze as Phase I of a longer-run economic stabilization program.

The adoption of the freeze as the initial stage of the stabilization policy seems to have been dictated by the need for a measure that could be imposed swiftly, before those affected by it could exploit the prospect of controls, and that would give the administration time to formulate a program better designed to meet long-run economic and equity needs—in short, to design what subsequently became Phase II of the economic stabilization program. It was also hoped, of course, that the freeze would alter, or begin to alter, the public's expectations with respect to inflation.

The newly created Cost of Living Council was to handle policy issues arising out of the implementation of the freeze. But since the freeze was only for ninety days, it was decided that exceptions and exemptions would be kept to a minimum. This left relatively few major policy issues to be decided.

---

[3] See *Economic Report of the President*, 1972 (Washington, D. C.: U.S. Government Printing Office, 1972), pp. 68-69.

As to wages and salaries, two of the most important questions to arise during the freeze concerned deferred increases and retroactive increases. The question of deferred increases—wage increases scheduled to become effective during the freeze, under the terms of collective bargaining contracts concluded before the freeze—involved a conflict between the legal status of contracts entered into in good faith and the principle of equity for nonunion workers who had no opportunity for deferred wage increases. The decision was to avoid discrimination and inconsistency by freezing *all* wages, regardless of the terms of existing contracts.[4]

The issue with respect to retroactive increases was how to deal with contracts which had expired before the freeze but had been settled during the freeze, with wage increases retroactive to the pre-freeze expiration date. Here, the Cost of Living Council agreed to permit retroactive payment of higher wages for work performed during the period between the contract expiration date and the beginning of the freeze (provided the parties could demonstrate that they had not changed their bargaining positions to offset the impact of the freeze), although retroactivity was not permitted for work performed during the freeze. The rationale for approving this limited retroactivity was that it would provide an incentive for reaching settlement in negotiations conducted during the freeze (the avoidance of strikes was an implicit goal of the stabilization program), and at the same time prevent "loading" the agreement to make up for the freeze.[5]

Both these decisions, it may be added, were hotly debated and modified when Phase I was replaced by Phase II—for organized labor, among others, had a fundamental stake in preserving the sanctity of contracts.

Besides dealing with issues of policy with respect to Phase I, the other major assignment of the Cost of Living Council during this period was the formulation of and preparation for Phase II.

Phase II

Objectives. As finally developed, Phase II was designed to meet not just one but several objectives, some of which tended to come into conflict with each other.

---

[4] See *Economic Stabilization Program, Quarterly Report Covering the Period August 15 Through December 31, 1971,* Cost of Living Council (Washington, D. C.: U.S. Government Printing Office, 1972), p. 6.

[5] Ibid., pp. 7-8.

The primary objective, of course, was to bring inflation under control. Accordingly, the interim target of Phase II was "to reduce the rate of inflation by about half, to a rate of 2 or 3 percent, by the end of 1972." At the same time, however, it was recognized that the program was not operating in a purely economic environment and that a variety of social, political and institutional factors had to be taken into consideration. So it was agreed that in addition to seeking to control inflation, the program must be fair and equitable, and should be designed to facilitate an "early" return to the free market economy and to interfere as little as possible with the operation of "normal market mechanisms." [6] This reflected a determination by the planners of Phase II to "prevent an undue strain on the institutions, contractual arrangements, and customary practices in the economy." [7] As far as the labor market was concerned, it meant permitting the normal processes of collective bargaining to operate with only the minimum intervention necessary to meet the anti-inflation objective, and it clearly meant restoring the legal status of collective bargaining contracts to the maximum degree possible.[8] But the question of the precise point at which contractual obligations had to yield to the imperatives of wage stabilization remained to be resolved.

The fact that Phase II had multiple objectives has at least one consequence that is often overlooked: its success or failure cannot be judged in terms of Pay Board standards alone, but must also be measured against the other objectives involved. But more on this point later.

Coverage. The general objectives outlined above led to the decision that Phase II should be mandatory rather than voluntary—and as comprehensive as possible to start with—both because the administration believed that experience with voluntary wage-price guideposts under the Kennedy-Johnson administrations had been unsatisfactory, and because it was feared that a voluntary program would be interpreted as the first move toward compulsory controls and would thus aggravate anticipatory price and wage increases.

As far as wages and salaries were concerned, two important general exemptions were announced by the Cost of Living Council before the Pay Board began to issue its general wage policies: wages below the federal minimum wage rate, and pay adjustments of

---

[6] *Economic Report of the President*, 1972, p. 83.

[7] *Economic Stabilization Program, Quarterly Report*, p. 23.

[8] *Economic Report of the President*, 1972, p. 83.

federal employees were exempt from the control program, although the administration requested that certain general pay increases for federal employees be postponed in the interests of conforming to the general standards of Phase II.

Additional reductions in the coverage of Phase II wage controls were subsequently provided by the low-wage and the small employer exemptions. The low-wage exemption originated in the December 1971 amendments to the Economic Stabilization Act, which provided that "substandard" wages and wages of the "working poor" should not be subject to control. On January 29, 1972, the Cost of Living Council announced that wages below $1.90 per hour would be considered substandard. Six months later, it raised the cut-off figure to $2.75 per hour; subsequently, during Phase III, the figure was raised to $3.50 by congressional mandate. The small employer exemption was issued on May 1, 1972, when the Cost of Living Council decided that most firms with sixty employees or less should not be subject to wage controls (firms with annual sales of $100,000 or less had already been exempted from price controls). These two exemptions thus involved a progressive narrowing of the coverage of Phase II wage controls. At the end of the first year of Phase II, the Cost of Living Council estimated that "roughly half of the work force" was exempted by the combination of the $2.75 low-wage standard and the small employer exemption.[9]

Administrative Categories of Controls. Early in the design of Phase II, it was decided that the program should concentrate on the largest economic units in the country. Indeed, this decision was hardly surprising, since it reflects the basic assumption of modern incomes policy, namely, that the success of controls depends upon restricting or restraining the market power of big firms and big unions.[10] Accordingly, in Category I, wage increases involving 5,000 or more workers (and price increases by firms with annual sales of $100 million or more) were subject to prenotification requirements—that is, they had to be reported to and approved by the Pay Board before being put into effect; in Category II, increases involving 1,000 workers or more had to be reported to the Pay Board; and in Cate-

---

[9] See supplemental submission of Judge George H. Boldt, Chairman of the Pay Board, in *Price and Wage Control: An Evaluation of Current Policies*, Hearings before the Joint Economic Committee, Congress of the United States, part 1, November 1972, p. 66.

[10] On this point, see Lloyd Ulman and Robert J. Flanagan, *Wage Restraint: A Study of Incomes Policy in Western Europe* (Berkeley: University of California Press, 1971), pp. 4-5.

gory III, those involving less than 1,000 workers were subject only to spot checks. Of these three categories, Category I involved some 10 percent of all employees, Category II, another 7 percent, and Category III, the remaining 83 percent.

The definitions of Category I and II—that is, wage increases involving 5,000 employees or more and 1,000 employees or more, respectively—were not arbitrary numbers picked out of thin air. Rather, these were statistical categories of long standing, and had been used by the Bureau of Labor Statistics (BLS) for many years in its analyses of collective bargaining agreements. The decision to use these categories as the basis for the wage control categories eliminated the need to reclassify BLS data and, at the same time, ensured much-needed continuity of wage data between precontrol and control periods.

The Pay Board. As the agency for administering the wage stabilization aspects of Phase II, a tripartite Pay Board was established, composed of fifteen members, five representing business, five organized labor, and five the public.

Tripartite composition. Although the board's composition might appear to be an administrative detail, it has long been recognized, both here and abroad, that no stabilization program will work, regardless of its substantive merits, unless it has the support of the major sectors of the community to whom it applies—in particular, labor and management. And perhaps the most effective way to secure and retain such support is to give these sectors participation, through representatives, in establishing the policies to which they will be subject. This point was explicitly recognized in the first report of the Economic Stabilization Program when it pointed out that:

> Economic decisions under the program would involve weighing the claims of participants in the economy and society in relation to the implications of these decisions for the progress in reducing inflation that was desired by and beneficial for all members in society. The participation of those representing major sectors of the economy and society was therefore built into the program to [bring to] bear on policy issues the expertise and interests of those affected by the operation of the program.[11]

Furthermore, it is worth noting that the concept of a tripartite stabilization agency goes back to the National War Labor Board of World War II and to its immediate predecessor, the National Defense

---

[11] *Economic Stabilization Program, Quarterly Report,* p. 25.

Mediation Board.[12] In addition, both of the wage stabilization agencies since then, the National Wage Stabilization Board (1945-1947) and the Wage Stabilization Board (1950-1953), were organized on a tripartite basis. The wage-price guideposts of the Kennedy administration were voluntary only, and no agency was ever established to administer them in the formal sense, although the Council of Economic Advisers fell heir to the principal responsibility for them.

Fundamentally, this tripartite organization reflects the fact—as Arnold Weber, a public member of the Pay Board, put it—that "the Pay Board has been established as a forum for national economic bargaining." [13] Viewed in this light, the determination of wage stabilization policy is an extension of collective bargaining between labor and management at the firm level to bargaining among labor, management, the administration, and the Congress over the content of national wage policy.

Similarly, the "walkout" of the majority of the labor members from the Pay Board, following the board's rejection of the longshoremen's contract in March 1972, may be seen as a strategic move in the overall bargaining between organized labor and the administration; having participated in the Pay Board's deliberations until its basic policies were completed,[14] the labor members felt they could then leave the board without jeopardizing their chance to affect its policies and, at the same time, put themselves in a position to require concessions from the administration to induce their return or renewed participation in the policy-making process. It is worth noting that the walkout was used by *both* labor and management members of the Wage Stabilization Board (1950-1963): the labor members withdrew in 1951 in protest against the board's wage policies (and returned again three months later), while the industry members and the board's chairman resigned in December 1952 in protest against President Truman's overruling a WSB decision.[15]

---

[12] For a careful analysis of the tripartite system, see W. Ellison Chalmers, Milton Derber, and William H. McPherson, as quoted in Gitlow, *Wage Determination Under National Boards*, p. 128.

[13] Arnold R. Weber, "Pay Board Problems, Seen From Inside," *Wall Street Journal*, February 8, 1972.

For a comparable analysis of the "game" of government policy determination, see Solomon Fabricant, "The Problem of Inflation," in National Bureau of Economic Research, Inc., *52nd Annual Report*, September 1972, pp. 18-19.

[14] Prepared statement of Judge Boldt in *Price and Wage Control: An Evaluation of Current Policies*, p. 10.

[15] See Gitlow, *Wage Determination Under National Boards*, pp. 184-185, 188. The chairman was Archibald Cox, now special prosecutor for the Justice Department in the Watergate case.

Wage policies: the general pay standard. The first policy decision of the Pay Board was to formulate its general pay standard, the
guideline for noninflationary increases in wages and benefits. It was
set at 5.5 percent, a figure predicated on the long-term trend increase
in productivity of 3.0 percent per year for the U.S. economy as a
whole, plus an increase of 2.5 percent per year to compensate for
the rate of price increase which the administration had set as its goal
for the first year of Phase II. In short, the 5.5 percent general pay
standard was designed to permit *real* compensation to rise in line with
trend productivity.

The 1962 wage guidepost, in contrast, made no allowance for
rising prices. It was designed to permit *money* wages, rather than
real wages, to rise in parallel with productivity. The 1971 general
pay standard may have been more equitable than the guideposts, in
that it afforded labor *some* protection against erosion of real wages
(full protection if the price target were met), and thus it may have
been more acceptable to organized labor.

The general pay standard was to be applicable to new labor
agreements or, in nonunion situations, to existing pay practices. And
in reviewing cases subject to the general pay standard, the board
indicated that it would consider "ongoing collective bargaining and
pay practices" and the equitable position of the employees involved,
including the impact of recent cost-of-living changes on their
compensation.

The general pay standard, it should be emphasized, applied to
"units," not to individual employees; it was the standard for the
permissible *average* increase for all employees covered by a collective
bargaining agreement, or subject to a particular wage decision. But
individual employees could receive increases in excess of the general
standard, as long as their increases were offset by less-than-standard
increases for other employees.

The general standard was designed, of course, to be a general
ceiling on permissible average wage increases, not a floor. Nonetheless,
the issuance of such a numerical standard has frequently been opposed
precisely because it is feared that, at least so far as negotiated wages
are concerned, it does become a floor, creating a situation in which
no union leader is willing, or politically able, to settle for less. Another
criticism is reflected in a February 1973 statement by the Labor-
Management Advisory Panel to the Cost of Living Council: "No single
standard of wage settlement can be equally applicable at one time
to all parties in an economy so large, decentralized and dynamic."[16]

---

[16] *New York Times*, February 27, 1973.

Wage policies: deferred and retroactive increases. At the same time as it decided on a general pay standard, the Pay Board was forced to grapple with issues first raised during the freeze, namely, deferred wage increases and retroactive wage increases.

Since the freeze was over, the objective of minimal interference in collective bargaining became a significant consideration in policy decisions. As a result, in a reversal from the Phase I policy on deferred increases, the legal status of contracts took precedence over trying to maintain equity as between union and nonunion employees. The Pay Board ruled that deferred increases should be granted, even though they exceeded the 5.5 percent general pay standard, unless challenged by a party to the agreement, or by five or more members of the board. If a deferred increase was challenged, the board would then determine whether or not it was "unreasonably inconsistent" with its criteria. The business members of the Pay Board subsequently indicated that they would challenge all deferred increases in excess of 7 percent, and this 7 percent limit eventually became accepted board policy.

The Council of Economic Advisers later estimated that if all known deferred increases scheduled for 1972 were limited to 7 percent, or less if the contract in question called for it, deferred increases would add "a little more than 0.1 percent to the average rate of wage increase for 1972." In other words, assuming the general pay standards were effective, it would bring the average increase in wages in the private sector to 5.6 percent.[17]

But when it came to retroactivity, the Pay Board opened the door only part way. It ruled that retroactive increases for work performed during the freeze would be permitted only upon board approval on a case by case basis, and that it would approve retroactivity only if (1) prices had been raised in anticipation of wage increases, (2) if a contract made during the freeze succeeded one that expired before the freeze, and retroactivity was an established practice or had been agreed to by the parties, or (3) severe inequities existed in the situation.[18]

These pay policies—the general pay standards and the policies regarding deferred and retroactive increases—were passed by a vote of ten to five, with the labor members dissenting. Afterward, AFL-CIO President Meany charged that these policies (on retroactive increases) "have abrogated our contracts." [19] As we shall see, having

---

[17] *Economic Report of the President,* 1972, p. 97.

[18] *Economic Stabilization Program, Quarterly Report,* p. 73.

[19] *New York Times,* November 9, 1971.

failed to win on the Pay Board, labor subsequently prevailed in Congress.

Wage policies: exceptions. Having enunciated its *general* pay standards, the Pay Board then moved on to deal with the problem of exceptions—those situations in which wage increases in excess of the general standards would be permitted. Basically, three major categories of exceptions were approved—(1) the tandem exception, involving relationships in which one or more agreements had historically been patterned on or followed a key collective bargaining situation, so that their wages moved in tandem with it; (2) the essential employee exception, involving wage increases needed to attract labor in certain labor shortage situations; and (3) the catch-up exception, involving situations in which wage increases in the three preceding years had totaled less than 7 percent. The maximum permissible increase, under any exception, or combination of exceptions, was 7 percent.[20]

Although these exceptions to the general pay standard resulted from the current decisions of the Pay Board, it should be emphasized that they were not simply the product of political and economic pressures of the moment, however great those pressures may have been. On the contrary, each of these policies followed a precedent established by a previous wage stabilization program. In recognizing that there had to be exceptions to its general pay standard to meet labor market needs, institutional needs, and considerations of equity and fairness, the Pay Board was adhering to the basic concepts of established wage stabilization policy.

As to the tandem exception, it has long been common in many industries for collective bargaining agreements in one major firm or group of firms to set a pattern that is followed closely by other firms so that wage and pay provisions in the latter quite literally move in tandem with those of the pattern-setter. But the establishment of the freeze on August 15, 1971, interfered with the operation of this relationship in a number of industries. In steel, for example, agreements were reached with the major steel companies in early August. But some of the smaller firms, which traditionally followed big steel by a matter of weeks, found their wages frozen and unable to move in accordance with their tandem pattern. Once Phase II began, it seemed appropriate and equitable to permit the steel companies caught in the freeze to raise wages by as much as 7 percent to restore their traditional tandem with the big steel com-

---

[20] *Economic Report of the President*, 1972, p. 92.

panies, so that a uniform pattern of wage increases in the steel industry would again prevail.

The tandem exception was not originally devised by the Pay Board. "General Wage Regulation 10—Tandems" was one of the main policies issued by the Wage Stabilization Board in 1951,[21] and it in turn grew out of the policies regarding interplant inequities developed by the National War Labor Board during World War II.

The essential employee exception permitted wage increases in excess of the general pay standard where necessary to attract labor in areas of labor shortage. Because such a policy contributes to effective allocation of labor, it serves the public interest as much as it does that of the parties directly involved. Accordingly, it was explicitly stated in the wage-price guidepost formula of 1962, by the Wage Stabilization Board of 1950 (although rarely), and by the National War Labor Board (although indirectly).[22]

The catch-up exception was designed to allow above-standard wage increases to workers who had fallen behind the pack in terms of wage increases, in order to bring them as nearly as possible into line with other employees. This exception was defined specifically to apply to cases where pay increases had aggregated less than 7 percent per year for the three preceding years and to allow whatever pay increase was necessary to bring their increases up to the 7 percent per year figure—even if it exceeded 5.5 percent. This exception expired November 14, 1972, at the end of the first year of Phase II.

The catch-up exception was recognized in both the wage-price guideposts and in General Wage Regulation 6 of the Wage Stabilization Board, which, as Chairman George Taylor of the WSB noted, meant simply that "Laggards had to be permitted to 'catch up' with 1950's wage trends."[23]

Parenthetically, it is interesting to note that the maximum deemed appropriate for the catch-up was 10 percent in 1950, as compared to 7 percent in 1972.

In addition, there was the gross inequities exception. Although this was not one of the three major exceptions announced by the board on December 17, 1971, the avoidance and correction of gross inequities was a fundamental part of Board policy. What constituted gross inequities had to be developed on a case-by-case basis.

[21] See Derber, "Wage Stabilization: Then and Now," p. 459.

[22] For these three cases see, respectively, *Economic Report of the President*, 1962, p. 189, and Gitlow, *Wage Determination Under National Boards*, pp. 208 and 153.

[23] Gitlow, *Wage Determination Under National Boards*, p. 204.

The 1971 Amendments to the Economic Stabilization Act. Since the statutory basis for controls, the Economic Stabilization Act of 1970, was due to expire at the end of April 1972, the administration asked Congress for a one-year extension of the act. On December 22, 1971, the Congress approved renewal of the law until April 30, 1973, but, in the process, it added five key amendments which substantially altered Pay Board policy and, as the administration complained, imposed some significant "constraints on the exercise (by the Administration) of authority under the Act." [24] The amendments illustrate two important aspects of the policy-making process in the wage stabilization program. First, they provide congressional input to the design of the program, both with respect to its basic goals and to its policies on specific issues. Second, they further illustrate the extent to which wage stabilization policies are the result of bargaining among the parties involved. In this case, organized labor, having failed to win approval of its case within the Pay Board (especially with respect to retroactivity), turned to the Congress and secured by legislation what it could not gain through the executive branch of the government.

Since the two issues of deferred and retroactive increases were perhaps the most controversial policy issues to face the wage stabilization authorities, both in Phase I and in the initial decisions of the Pay Board, it is not surprising that they were the subject of the first of the amendments to the Economic Stabilization Act. Indeed, the fact that so much attention had to be given these issues by the Cost of Living Council, the Pay Board and the Congress is a measure both of the impact of the freeze on the customary practices and institutions in the labor market and of the substantial efforts made to adjust and correct them.

The five amendments mandated the following policies: [25]

1. Deferred increases negotiated before the freeze and scheduled to take effect after the freeze were to be paid, unless "unreasonably inconsistent" with Pay Board standards.
2. Perhaps more important, deferred increases negotiated before the freeze and scheduled to take effect during the freeze, but not paid because of the freeze, were now to be paid *retroactively*, unless "unreasonably inconsistent" with the board's standards. Prior to this amendment, increases foregone because of the freeze were permitted to be restored only

---

[24] *Economic Stabilization Program, Quarterly Report*, p. 29.

[25] See *Economic Report of the President*, 1972, p. 95. For the text of the amendments, see *Economic Stabilization Program, Quarterly Report*, p. 145.

if approved by the Pay Board, under any of three criteria; now, the burden was shifted, so that they would be paid *unless disapproved* by the board. Further, if law or contracts existing before August 15 had called for increases during the freeze, they were to be paid retroactively, regardless of Pay Board standards, if funds had been raised to cover them, prices advanced, or productivity increased.

3. A variety of fringe benefits, such as employer contributions to pensions, group insurance and health plans, were ordered excluded from the definition of "wages and salaries" for control purposes, unless "unreasonably inconsistent" with the standards for wages, salaries and prices. In other words, these so-called "qualified benefits" were not to be counted as part of a wage increase in calculating whether or not it was within the general pay standards or the official exceptions.

As a result of this amendment, the Pay Board subsequently established a 0.7 percent increase standard for these "qualified" benefits, so that instead of a 5.5 percent general pay standard, the general standard for total compensation became 6.2 percent—5.5 percent plus 0.7 percent.[26] In addition, exceptions to the standard increase for qualified benefits allowed catch-ups in qualified benefits up to a maximum of 1.5 percent, for a total of 2.2 percent.

Taking all permissible exceptions together, a unit could be permitted total increases as high as 12 percent in a single control year (the administrative period involved).[27]

4. Individuals whose wages were "substandard" or who were "members of the working poor" were not subject to wage controls—until their earnings rose above the "substandard" level or they were no longer a member of the "working poor." Having stated this policy, however, the Congress thoughtfully left the definition of these terms to the Pay Board and the Cost of Living Council.

This assignment proved to be a major problem for these agencies. The Cost of Living Council (rather than the Pay Board) first established a wage rate of $1.90 an hour as the dividing line between "standard" and "substandard" wages although the Pay Board had previously rejected this figure as too low.[28] But in July 1972, after a major union went to

---

[26] See prepared statement of Judge Boldt in *Price and Wage Control: An Evaluation of Current Policies*, p. 14.
[27] Ibid., p. 9.
[28] *New York Times*, January 29, 1972.

court to challenge this ruling and won its case, the Cost of Living Council revised its low-wage standard to $2.75 an hour. And when the Economic Stabilization Act came up for its third renewal in April 1973, Congress set the low-wage standard at $3.50 an hour, effective May 1, 1973.

These successively higher low-wage exemptions did more than give aid and comfort to workers receiving substandard wages, for each increase narrowed the coverage of the economic stabilization program. After the Cost of Living Council raised the low-wage exemption to $2.75 an hour, the Pay Board estimated that at $2.75 an hour about two-thirds, and at $3.50 an hour about half, of all nonsupervisory workers in the private nonfarm sector would remain subject to controls, although some had already been removed from controls because of being subject to the "small employer exemption." [29]

The Construction Industry Stabilization Committee. Because the Construction Industry Stabilization Committee, the Nixon administration's first experiment with wage controls, had been established nearly nine months prior to Phase II and had developed both policy and expertise with respect to the problems of the construction industry, the Pay Board in effect made CISC its agent for carrying out stabilization policies in the construction industry. Subsequently, what amounted to a jurisdictional agreement between the two was reached, which gave the CISC control over all *union* wages and the Pay Board control over *nonunion* wages in construction.[30]

Furthermore, it was recognized that CISC wage policies need not be identical with those of the Pay Board, but should "conform as closely as the special conditions of the construction industry permit to those of the Pay Board." [31] Accordingly, unlike the Pay Board, CISC has never issued a general numerical pay standard for permissible wage increases, nor automatically approved pay increases up to 5.5 percent. Instead, it operates on an essentially case-by-case basis, on the theory that what constitutes a settlement meeting the requirements of both equity and wage stabilization depends on the circumstances of each case.

[29] See supplemental submission of Judge Boldt in *Price and Wage Control: An Evaluation of Current Policies*, p. 66.

[30] Pay Board release, June 9, 1972.

[31] See D. Quinn Mills, "Wage Stabilization in the Construction Industry: An Historical Perspective," *Labor Law Journal*, August 1972, p. 466.

The Construction Industry Stabilization Committee approach to wage stabilization took on added significance after January 1, 1973, when Phase II gave way to Phase III and John T. Dunlop, who had been the chairman of CISC, became the director of the Cost of Living Council. From January 11, 1973, to June 8, 1973, when the President announced a new freeze on prices and plans for Phase IV, no specific new wage guidepost for Phase III was announced. Yet despite frequent criticism, and despite the administration's eventual admission that Phase III had been generally unsuccessful, the one area in which moderation was apparent was in collective bargaining settlements. Indeed, it was because of the relatively satisfactory performance of wages during Phase III that they were not included in the June 8 freeze order.

Other Special Situations. Special problems and special methods of dealing with them also existed in several other cases.

Federal government employees. The wages and salaries of federal employees were not subject to Pay Board regulations. Instead, the Federal Pay Agent (the administrative agency within the executive branch) was to monitor federal pay to ensure consistency with the stabilization program, and the Cost of Living Council was to advise the President as to the consistency of federal pay decisions with the stabilization program. The reason for this seems clear enough. Stabilization efforts had previously been hurt by the example of federal pay increases taking effect when employees in the private sector were being asked—or required—to forgo increases in the name of public interest. Some mechanism for avoiding a repetition of such occurrences was clearly needed.

In accordance with this policy, the President proposed as the equivalent of the wage freeze of August 15, a six-month deferral in the federal pay increase scheduled to take effect on January 1, 1972.[32] This proposal was announced on August 15 as part of the New Economic Policy. The Congress, however, refused to go along, and the pay increase became effective January 1 as scheduled.[33]

State and local government employees. Their pay was made subject to Pay Board regulations, but advance notice of pay increases was waived; and if the governmental unit involved agreed to abide by Pay Board standards, it could report semiannually.[34] In addition, a Committee of State and Local Government Cooperation was estab-

---

[32] *Economic Report of the President,* 1972, p. 70.

[33] Ibid., p. 71.

[34] Ibid., p. 92.

lished to deal with such special problems of this sector as retroactive pay for teachers whose salaries were frozen during the period August 15-November 14, 1971, automatic wage progressions for these employees, and the need for a separate wage category for such public employees.[35]

Executives. Late in December 1971, the Pay Board announced its policies as to executive and incentive compensation not covered by collective bargaining agreements: basically such compensation was required to conform to the 5.5 percent general pay standard. The board indicated that its policies, which were based on recommendations of a special committee on executive compensation, represented the strongest control of executive wages and salaries ever issued by the federal government.[36]

Health service industry employees. The wage policies covering employees in the health service industries were formulated by the Health Services Industry Committee of the Pay Board. Its wage subcommittee recommended adherence to the 5.5 percent general pay standard, except for workers receiving less than $2.00 per hour, who should be allowed increases up to 8 percent.[37]

Pay Board Actions. At the end of its first year of operation, the Pay Board had completed action on over 10,000 cases. Beginning with its early key cases on bituminous coal and the railroad signalmen (in which it awarded increases considerably above its general pay standard and was roundly criticized for it), through the aerospace cases (when it first rejected a newly negotiated wage increase) and the longshoremen's case (which provoked four of the five labor members to walk off), the board had to consider the particular circumstances of each case before it, determine which policy or combination of policies from the complex of standards and exceptions outlined above was applicable, and then judge how much of an increase was permissible. And the decision as to what wage increase should be permitted depended not only on the board's judgment in each particular case, but on what criteria or combination of criteria the facts of the case met. This was a function, in part, of the composition of the pay package submitted for approval, which in turn might have been as much a product of previous negotiations as of the current one. Under these circumstances, it is impossible to judge how "strict"

---

[35] *Economic Stabilization Program, Quarterly Report,* pp. 81-90.

[36] *Economic Report of the President,* 1972, p. 83.

[37] *Economic Stabilization Program, Quarterly Report,* p. 92.

or how "easy" the board was simply by how close it came to the 5.5 percent general pay standard of Phase II.

Phase III

On January 11, 1973, after stabilization officials had spent a month consulting with public officials, congressional leaders and representatives of various interest groups, President Nixon announced the third phase of the Economic Stabilization Program.

Phase III involved a shift of emphasis among anti-inflation weapons, with wage and price controls being eased, and major reliance being placed on fiscal policy and a tighter rein on federal spending. In addition, Phase III involved a shift from mandatory controls to self-regulation or, as the administration expressed it, self-administration. Except in the construction, food, and health industries, which remained under mandatory controls, prior approval of changes in wages and prices was no longer required. In general, compliance with noninflationary standards was to be voluntary, although the federal government retained the power—"the stick in the closet" as it came to be known—to restore mandatory controls as necessary to prevent serious breaches of the anti-inflation standards. As far as wages were concerned, it was indicated that the general pay standards of Phase II would be the guides for voluntary compliance, pending a review and possible change by a newly created Labor-Management Advisory Committee.

Both the Pay Board and the Price Commission were disbanded. Their functions were absorbed by the Cost of Living Council, under its new director, John Dunlop.

Although the rising levels of economic activity in late 1972 convinced many economists that controls designed for cost-push inflation were no longer appropriate, Phase III proved to be ill-timed, for it coincided with a renewed surge of inflation. The seasonally adjusted annual rate of increase in the consumer price index, after having been only 3.2 percent in the fourth quarter of 1972, reached 8.8 percent in the first quarter of 1973, while the increase in the wholesale price index reached 21.1 percent. In both cases, these were the largest increases for any quarter since 1951. Food prices—the major source of the rise in the CPI—rose at a seasonally adjusted annual rate of 29.8 percent, also the largest quarterly gain since 1951. International reaction was severe, and provoked such a massive outflow of dollars that the secretary of the treasury announced a devaluation of the dollar on February 12, 1973. The net result of this monetary crisis was that

125

the U.S. balance-of-payments position deteriorated sharply, with the deficit rising from $1.5 billion in the fourth quarter of 1972 to $10.5 billion in the first quarter of 1973.

Yet quite clearly, wages were not a significant factor in the renewed surge of inflation in the first half of 1973. In fact, their behavior is further evidence that the current inflation is the result of excess demand rather than of cost-push forces. Increases in collective bargaining settlements in 1973-I were generally the smallest they had been in some time. Wage increases over the life of the contract in that quarter were the smallest in four years—wages and benefits rose an average of 5.5 percent, and wages only, 4.5 percent. In the case of first-year adjustments the increase of 7.3 percent in wages and benefits was the same as that for the last quarter of 1972, while in the case of wages only, the 5.3 percent rise was the lowest in four years.

In the private nonfarm sector, adjusted average hourly earnings rose 5.0 percent in 1973-I, the second smallest gain since before the freeze in 1971-III. And while compensation per man-hour rose by 10.8 percent in 1973-I, as compared to 6.5 percent in 1972-IV its sudden surge was due mainly to an increase in the employers' social security payroll tax, rather than to private decisions.

The 1973 Price Freeze and Phase IV

As a consequence of their moderate behavior wages were not included when on June 13, 1973, almost six months to the day after he had announced Phase III, the President ordered a freeze on all prices except those of unprocessed farm products at the farm and rents, as a prelude to Phase IV.

In many ways, the freeze of June 1973 resembled the freeze of August 1971. In both cases, it was announced that the freeze was temporary, in order to give the administration time to design post-freeze controls; in both cases the freeze had been preceded by a balance-of-payments crisis, by unacceptably rapid increases in prices (though price increases were sharper in 1973 than in 1971), and by a public clamor for stronger anti-inflation measures.

But there were also significant differences in the circumstances prevailing at the introduction of the two freezes. In mid-1971, there was considerable slack in the economy, as indicated by both an unemployment rate of 5.8 percent in June 1971 and a capacity utilization rate of 75 percent in manufacturing in the June quarter of 1971. In 1973, on the other hand, the unemployment rate had leveled off at 5.0 percent for three months preceding the freeze, and the economy was running at over 80 percent of capacity. There was still some slack, but it was less than existed when the Phase I freeze was introduced.

When Phase IV was announced on July 18, 1973, the general wage and benefit guidelines in effect during Phase II and Phase III were continued.

What Happened to Wages during Controls? [38]

Now that Phases I and II are completed, and (at this writing) Phase III is about to be succeeded by Phase IV, the obvious question is: what happened to wages during Phase I and Phase II? And while we can report more or less accurately the behavior of wages during Phase I and Phase II, the extent to which that behavior was a *result* of controls is likely to be debated for some time to come, as was the question of whether wage-price guideposts were effective in reducing wages from 1962 to 1966. So we confine ourselves here to reporting *what* happened to wages during the first two phases of controls, without confronting the question of *why* they behaved as they did.

Wages under Collective Bargaining. Of greatest interest, perhaps, is what happened to negotiated wages under controls. The size and continued acceleration of negotiated wage increases in the face of economic slowdown in 1970 and 1971 were important factors in the decision to impose wage controls in 1971 (whereas the fact that negotiated wages were generally rising more and more slowly doubtless influenced the decision to exempt wages from the freeze announced June 13, 1973).

If we use 1971-III as our base we get a measure of change for the period most nearly corresponding to Phase II—although it may tend to overstate the apparent success of controls, since wage increases in 1971-III were considerably above the previous trend. In 1972-IV, at what was virtually the end of Phase II, BLS data show that first-year adjustments in negotiated wages for all industries were slightly less than half what they had been in 1971-III (Table 1). This is true for first-year adjustments of both wages alone, which fell from

[38] The material in this section is largely a revision of material and data in my "Wage Policy in Phase II: A Preliminary Appraisal," *Proceedings* of the 25th Annual Meeting of the Industrial Relations Research Association, 1972, pp. 15-22.

Table 1

WAGE CHANGES DURING CONTROLS

(quarter-to-quarter changes; percent change over previous quarter at annual rate)

Item	1971				1972				1973	
	I	II	III	IV	I	II	III	IV	I	II
Negotiated wages, first-year adjustments										
Wages and benefits, 5,000 workers or more	10.6	11.5	15.0	12.7	9.7	8.1	8.7	7.3	7.3	7.6
Wages only, 1,000 workers or more, all industries	10.0	10.4	13.5	10.5	8.7	7.1	7.6	6.4	5.3	6.1
Wages only, construction	18.0	13.1	12.3	11.5	19.0	6.3	6.4	4.3	4.5	6.3
General wage measures, private nonfarm economy										
Average hourly compensation a		7.9	6.8	4.7	9.8	5.2	6.4	6.5	10.8	6.0
Average hourly earnings adjusted b		7.0	6.4	4.8	8.3	5.6	5.3	7.1	5.0	6.4

a Average hourly compensation, all employees, in current dollars.
b Adjusted for overtime (in manufacturing only) and for inter-industry shifts.

Source: Wage and benefit decisions data from *Review of Productivity, Wages, Prices, and Employment* (second quarter, 1973), Bureau of Labor Statistics release, August 3, 1973, Table 7; general wage measures, data from *ibid.,* Table 5.

13.5 percent to 6.4 percent, and wages and benefits, which eased from 15.0 percent to 7.3 percent.

If on the other hand we use the pre-freeze quarter of 1971-II as the base, it may understate the impact of controls, because it ignores the peak quarter of 1971-III. Here we find that by 1972-IV, first-year adjustments were roughly one-third less than they had been in 1971-II. First-year adjustments in wages alone were down from 10.4 percent to 6.4 percent, and in wages and benefits, down from 11.5 percent to 7.3 percent.

But whether we measure the changes from 1971-II or 1971-III, it is clear that during Phase I and Phase II there was a substantial reduction in the rate of increase of negotiated wages. While the size of negotiated adjustments increased in 1973-II, the second quarter of Phase II, it is too early to know whether this marks the beginning of an acceleration in negotiated wage increases.

It is interesting to note that except in construction, first-year adjustments in union settlements (both wages only and benefits) lack the post-freeze "bubble" evident in both average hourly earnings and in compensation per man-hour data. Thus, after rising in 1971-III, the quarter in which general wage controls were introduced, first-year wage adjustments declined for three consecutive quarters, rose slightly in 1972-III, and declined again in 1972-IV. And although first-year construction contracts rose by 19.0 percent in 1972-I, only 32,000 workers were involved and their impact on overall collective bargaining data was negligible.

No evaluation of the behavior of negotiated wages under control is complete, of course, without considering the special case of construction. This industry has been subject to wage controls longer than other industries and, prior to controls, had recorded the most rapid rate of wage increase of any unionized industry. In 1972-IV, first-year wage adjustments in major construction contracts were 4.3 percent—roughly one-third what they had been in 1971-III, and approximately one-quarter of their 18.0 percent average in 1971-I, just prior to the establishment of the Construction Industry Stabilization Committee.

What is perhaps more significant about the construction industry stabilization program, however, is that since its inception we have moved from a situation in which major construction settlements *raised* the average size of *all* major collective bargaining settlements to one in which their effect is to *lower* that average. Thus in 1970, first-year wage adjustments in major construction agreements not only reached a level nearly double those in all other industries—in

129

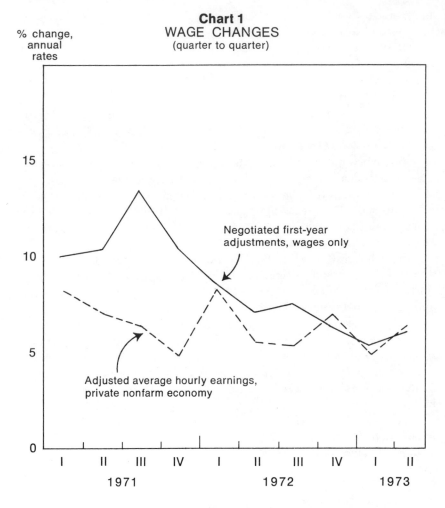

Chart 1
WAGE CHANGES
(quarter to quarter)

% change,
annual
rates

Negotiated first-year
adjustments, wages only

Adjusted average hourly earnings,
private nonfarm economy

15

10

5

0

I   II   III   IV   I   II   III   IV   I   II

1971   1972   1973

1970-III, construction settlements averaged 21.3 percent, and all other industries, 10.8 percent—but raised the all-industry average for the full year 1970 from 10.9 percent to 11.9 percent, or by roughly nine percent. In 1972-IV, on the other hand, after twenty-one months under controls, first-year construction settlements averaged 4.3 percent, compared to an average of 6.4 percent for all industries.

General Wage Changes in the Private Nonfarm Sector. General wage behavior in the private nonfarm sector during Phases I and II was quite different from that of negotiated wages. Since the rate of increase of both average hourly compensation and average hourly earnings declined in 1971-III, one quarter before the slowdown in

130

negotiated wage increases, their changes during controls are less pronounced. Thus the rate of increase of average hourly compensation in 1972-IV was only 20 percent less than it had been in 1971-II, while average hourly earnings rose slightly more in 1972-IV than in either 1971-II or 1971-III.

By the end of Phase II, after seventeen months of controls, there had been a substantially greater decline in the size of increases in negotiated wages than of increases in average hourly compensation, while increases in average hourly earnings had remained virtually unchanged. While this may mean that controls had more impact on negotiated wages than on wage changes generally, it may also reflect the fact that union wages, as usual, are slower to respond to changing economic circumstances than other compensation, and that the rise in average hourly compensation and in average hourly earnings in the last half and the last quarter of 1972, respectively, reflects their quicker response to expanding economic activity.

Pay Board Data. If the BLS data give us the best measures of the rate at which wages are changing, the Pay Board data provide a snapshot of a considerably broader area than the BLS measures of major collective bargaining settlements. In particular, the Pay Board's figures cover both union and nonunion settlements, and increases in some portions of the public sector (notably public education) as well as the private sector. By the end of Phase II, on January 11, 1973, the board had approved pay packages in Category I and Category II cases involving 23,119,000 employees, of whom 51.4 percent were under collective bargaining and 48.6 percent nonunion.[39]

Union settlements. The Pay Board reports that between November 14, 1971, and January 11, 1973, the average of approved first-year increases in union cases involving 1,000 workers or more was 6.9 percent and the average of deferred increases was 5.6 percent, for a weighted average of 5.9 percent. This compares with the weighted average for all Pay Board cases during this period of 5.3 percent. In addition, the Construction Industry Stabilization Committee reports that, in construction, the average of approved first-year increases from November 14, 1971, to December 31, 1972, was 5.9 percent, and of deferred increases, 5.5 percent—in both cases, smaller percentage increases than the Pay Board average for all union situations.[40]

---

[39] All Pay Board data from *Economic Stabilization Program, Quarterly Report, Covering the Period October 1, 1972, Through January 10, 1973,* Cost of Living Council (Washington, D. C.: U.S. Government Printing Office, 1973), p. 48.
[40] CISC Press Release, June 11, 1973.

Nonunion settlements. In nonunion cases, as one might expect, the average increase approved by the Pay Board was considerably less than in union cases. The combined average for new and deferred increases was 4.7 percent.

Wages, Productivity and Unit Labor Costs. During the period of controls, the rate of wage increase has slowed significantly, particularly for negotiated increases. But when it comes to cutting labor costs, effective wage restraint is only one blade of the scissors—the other is productivity growth. Both are crucial to the fight on inflation. It is significant, therefore, that following two years of little productivity growth in 1969 and 1970, productivity gains in 1971 and 1972 have been substantial, rising above the 3.0 percent long-term growth rate in both the total private economy and the private nonfarm sector. In 1971, output per man-hour in the private nonfarm economy was up 3.6 percent from the previous year, as against 0.6 percent in 1970 and in 1972, it rose 4.7 percent.

This sharp productivity gain, combined with an easing in the growth of compensation per man-hour, resulted in an almost 50 percent reduction in the rate of gain in unit labor costs in the private nonfarm sector, from 6.6 percent in 1970 to 3.4 percent in 1971. And in 1972, unit labor costs in the private nonfarm sector not only stopped rising, but actually declined in the second and third quarters, with the net result that for 1972 as a whole, unit labor costs rose only 1.7 percent, the smallest rise since 1965. It is worth noting that a larger part of this improvement in unit labor costs has been due to acceleration in productivity than to deceleration of compensation.

But past experience suggests that the current rate of productivity growth cannot be sustained, and that a slowdown from the present high rates of growth may be expected in 1973, and along with it some rise in unit labor costs. In fact, in 1973-II, the rate of productivity actually declined by 0.3 percent, and unit labor costs were up 5.9 percent. When productivity eases, restraint on the rate of increase in compensation will become more rather than less critical if inflationary pressures on the cost side are to be controlled.

Conclusion

The apparent success of Phase II wage and price controls posed a dilemma for the administration. Although the slowdown in wage and price increases was a welcome move toward its goal of bringing inflation under control, the popular belief that it resulted from controls was disconcerting to an administration philosophically opposed to controls and eager to end them as soon as possible. And if Phase II contributed to the belief that controls "worked," surely the belief was reinforced when the relaxation of controls in Phase III was accompanied by a renewed acceleration of prices and by the decision to return to tougher controls in Phase IV. Whether the public thus learned "all the wrong lessons," as the *Wall Street Journal* maintained, is another question,[41] but there is little doubt that these *were* the lessons learned.

Quite aside from this dilemma, the problem of trying to evaluate how successful wage controls were during Phase I and Phase II is complicated by a variety of factors. First, it should be recognized that in fact there have been two wage stabilization programs—one for the construction industry and the other for the rest of the economy. Although they are related both administratively and by a substantial area of common policy, there are distinct differences in their approach and policy for wage stabilization, as we have shown.[42]

Second, it is clear that there was a considerable slowdown in the rate of *negotiated* wage increases under both the construction and the general wage stabilization programs (though the picture is less clear so far as overall wages are concerned). One must admit, however, that it is impossible to be certain how much of this slowdown, if any, was due to controls. Yet we concur with the judgment of the Council of Economic Advisers that "it is probable that the controls did reduce the rate of inflation." [43]

Finally, it must be remembered that although the primary goal of wage stabilization was to combat inflation, the program also sought to maintain equity and fairness and to minimize disruption to "normal market mechanisms" such as collective bargaining. There are no statistical measures of the effectiveness of the wage stabilization program in maintaining or protecting equities or in preserving the free collective bargaining process, and no standard against which to measure effectiveness.

All of which serves to emphasize again that wage stabilization is a form of national economic bargaining and that it is therefore an exercise in *political economy*, rather than in economics, per se. Accordingly, its effectiveness can never be measured in terms of its economic impact alone. Eventually it must be judged in qualitative as well as in quantitative terms. At this time, we are too close to the events—indeed, they are still taking place—to make such a judgment. That judgment must await another day.

[41] *Wall Street Journal*, April 9, 1973.
[42] See pp. 122-123.
[43] *Economic Report of the President*, 1973, p. 61.

5

EMPLOYMENT GOALS AND MONETARY-FISCAL OVEREXPANSION

William Fellner

This study discusses the question of realistic employment-rate targets; the nature of the inflationary instability that developed in the second half of the sixties when the economy was driven to unsustainable levels; the importance of avoiding a repetition of that experience over an extended period; the difficulties arising from the fact that by now— only about two years after the recession of 1970—we have already experienced a short period of overheating which coincided with further complications originating in the raw-materials sector; and the problem of policy measures available for preventing a prolongation of this imbalance and for thus avoiding a severe recession, even at the risk of a minor setback.

Note on the Price Freeze Announced after Completion of the Study

On June 13, 1973, President Nixon announced a price freeze lasting up to sixty days, with a "Phase IV" control program for the subsequent period to be worked out in the interim. This study was completed prior to that announcement. As the reader will see, I have argued that any attempt to deal with the inflation problem in this fashion would be quite ill-advised. Even prior to June 13, we all were aware that in some circles the step that has now been taken was regarded as "good politics"—even though those holding this view would have had a hard time refuting the proposition that trying to cope with an excess-demand situation in this way is "bad economics." I find it difficult to imagine that the step will not also prove to be "bad politics."

In 1972 the economic policies that determine subsequent aggregate demand were much too expansionary, and a number of special supply-limiting factors became significant. If the basic demand-supply discrepancy is allowed to continue, then price-control measures purporting to be "anti-inflationary" can do no more than to suppress *symptoms*; and to do *even this* effectively, such measures would have to be enforced ruthlessly and supplemented by a system of allocations and rationing for which both public opinion and the administrative apparatus are wholly unprepared. It is fortunate that they should be unprepared, because perpetuating shortages and rigidifying an economy by price controls and rationing can hardly be considered a desirable objective. If, on the other hand, policy makers will adopt the necessary measures for moderating the increase in demand and for promoting the increase in supply, then it is essential that they should allow changes in the price structure, as determined by market forces, to guide the required output adjustments. In one's more optimistic moments, one can only remind oneself that the authorities are not yet committed to any large-scale interference with the price structure beyond a very limited period.

Overexpansion combined with attempts to treat the resulting malady by outlawing its symptoms is a dangerous course. Unfortunately the number of those who see this clearly and also have the courage of their convictions has proved disappointingly small. The reader will notice that when my study was written there was reason to fear such a regrettable outcome, but not to take it for granted. However, the study calls for no modification because the basic problems remain those to which the following pages are addressed.

Overview

Employment-Rate Targets and the Speed of Approaching Them. In my earlier studies in the present series I argued that the prospect of keeping the American rate of inflation low during the coming years—indeed the prospect of preventing a renewed significant acceleration of inflation—would depend largely on whether expansionary monetary and fiscal policy *stopped short* of reducing our overall unemployment rate below about 5 percent. I argued that expansionary policies are unsuitable means of dealing with hardship cases remaining at the 5 percent unemployment level. This would have been the case even aside from the specific problem of primary product prices which has recently started to become disturbing. In actual fact, specific difficulties originating on the supply side of raw material markets, as well as capacity shortages, have recently led to a renewed flare-up of inflation even before our unemployment rate would have declined below 5 percent. But at 5 percent we would have been very near the danger zone in any event.

When the overall unemployment rate as estimated by conventional American methods is in the neighborhood of 5 percent, the labor market for major specific categories of workers becomes distinctly tight and, although other categories of workers still have high unemployment rates, this problem cannot be solved by "pumping up" the economy further. The data I used in my earlier studies strongly pointed in this direction, and so do the more recent data, all of which suggest also that shifts in the composition of the labor force have played a large role in changing the nature of the employment policy problem since the nineteen-fifties. Some of our policy makers surely realize this. How many of them believe that, given the political pressures, they can afford to be guided by this insight is a question about which I am less clear. The answer cannot be found in their statements because for a responsible person in public life it is even more difficult to *state* openly that he is guided by such an insight than to be guided by it *in fact*. Whenever a political personality has touched on this subject he has been sharply criticized for "redefining" full employment instead of getting us there. Some at least have stood up well under the pressure, but nevertheless by the late part of 1972 far too much expansionary momentum had been built into the economy. Up to the recent significant intensification of inflationary pressures expansionary monetary and fiscal policy were directed at more ambitious goals than those consistent with the analysis to be presented here.

There is reason to believe that the emphasis deserves to be placed on the height of employment-rate targets, not simply on how rapidly or how slowly we approach them. Sometimes it is suggested that when labor market tightness at low unemployment rates (high employment rates) *appears* to result from an insufficient supply of workers in highly demanded worker categories, the *true* reason for the observed symptoms is not the low level of unemployment, but its rate of decline. According to this argument, which I find unconvincing, a too rapid decline in the unemployment rate—for example, the decline of 0.9 percentage points from December 1964 to December 1965 and again in a later twelve-month period—may overstrain the adaptability of the system whereas a slower decline would not. It is quite true that rates of change and adaptability play a large role in the maintenance or loss of balance, because excess capacities cannot be coordinated and put in working condition overnight. But the orders of magnitude greatly weaken any analogous reasoning when it becomes focused on the wage-raising effect of intensified competition for labor.

This is so because, during the inflationary years with which we shall be concerned, the periods of rapidly declining unemployment were periods in which the civilian labor force would have increased by at least 2 percent a year even with a smaller decline of unemployment. During 1965, the year of the sixties when inflation started accelerating, man-hour input in the private economy rose by slightly over 3 percent. It might have increased by, say, 2½ percent, if the unemployment rate had declined by less than the observed 0.9 percent. Now, it is quite true that in this hypothetical case the demand for labor would have been smaller in 1965 and the wage increases—which for some time were registering tightness particularly for non-union workers—would have been less pronounced. But if *that* one-half percentage point increase in labor input which thus would not have taken place in 1965 had been postponed and added on to the increase of the next period—that is, if the decrease of unemployment had been spread in this fashion—then subsequently the competition of employers for workers would have been even more intense than was actually the case. Therefore wages would subsequently have risen even faster than they actually did (though from a lower base). It is unclear why such a course of events would have diminished, rather than merely *postponed*, the full wage-raising effect of labor-market tightness—except on the assumption that the need to hire much additional labor in a hurry prevents proper exploration of the labor market and hence leads to an irreversible overpayment of workers. It would be farfetched to build heavily on this latter assumption when it comes to comparing a 2½ percent a year increase in labor input with a 3 percent increase. What mattered in the labor market conditions typified by 1965 was primarily the limited availability of various kinds of labor, not the greater wage-raising effect of more awkward hiring practices when during a twelve-month span about 3 percent was added to the labor input instead of about 2½ percent.

Recent Raw Material Shortages. Yet with respect to the past few quarters and the immediate future, it is necessary to pay attention not merely to what would be *overexpanded demand* even under normal conditions, but also to another problem. After all, during 1972 we were merely approaching the 5 percent unemployment rate from above, and policy makers can rightly point to a favorable general consumer price record for that year. Another problem developed as a result of factors affecting the *supply side* of commodity markets, and manifesting themselves in rapidly rising raw material prices, particularly the steep rise in the prices of farm products. During the year 1972 these pressures showed up to a significant extent only in the farm-products and raw-materials components of the wholesale price index. Subsequently they started showing up dramatically in the general wholesale index and the consumer price index, too, both of which rose exceedingly steeply in the first quarter of 1973.

The assumption seems justified that, other things equal, much the greater part of these price increases would merely create a temporary complication, with a more lasting effect developing mainly from the rising prices of raw materials needed for the production of energy. Other things equal, most of the difficulty would be temporary, partly because recent crop failures abroad, particularly in the U.S.S.R., have led to *exceptionally* large American grain exports, and partly because constructive measures have been taken to increase American farm acreages, to relax various import restrictions and to make it more difficult and more expensive to keep large inventories of certain farm products. Furthermore, the depreciation in the value of the dollar is apt to express itself in a greater short-run than long-run increase in the domestic price level. However, if by the temporary problem we mean major increases in the cost of living induced by factors affecting the supply of raw materials, then this problem is apt to last, in any event, into the second half of 1973. The danger is that otherwise "temporary" steep price increases that nevertheless last for a good many months may become built into current cost trends—particularly into wage trends. If this happens on a major scale, an otherwise temporary effect might well become long-lasting. In this case "other things" would not remain equal in the sense implied above.

Direct Controls. Whether wage and price controls were effective at the low employment rates prevailing in 1971 and during much of 1972 will always remain a controversial question. A persuasive case can be made for stressing market forces rather than the controls to explain the flattening of price trends that occurred at that time. But whatever the uncertainties of diagnosis may be for that period—a period with significant slack in the economy—it would surely be a mistake to expect good results from direct controls for moderating the demand pressures we are facing in the *present* phase of expansion.

139

So far we have gone through a three-month period of price and wage freeze (Phase I beginning on August 15, 1971), then through a longer period with extensive and arbitrary interferences in the price structure (Phase II lasting until January 1973),[1] and more recently we moved into a period of more relaxed controls (Phase III). At the present writing very strong political pressure is being exerted to have the administration adopt much tighter controls once more. Yet what our difficulties call for is not such an effort to suppress symptoms by methods that interfere with the needed supply adjustments but a policy of preventing aggregate demand from running ahead of supply.

Reasonable Growth Target for 1973. During the last quarter of 1972 the seasonally corrected overall unemployment rate was about 5¼ percent on the average; by December it had declined to 5.1 percent, by January 1973 to 5.0 percent, and by June 1973 to 4.8 percent. In the first quarter of 1973 capacity utilization rates were very high in a considerable number of industries.

Quite aside from our temporary farm products problem and other raw-material shortages, expansionary policies should not have been used in such a way as to raise the economy's real growth rate from the last quarter of 1972 to that of 1973 much beyond the sum of the increase in the labor force and in output per man-hour. This sum should be estimated with merely a small allowance for any further post-recession "catching up" of these magnitudes after the last quarter of 1972. For the economy as a whole the sum may be 5 percent at most, and it probably is somewhat less. Leaving a very small amount of room for cyclical expansion from the last quarter of 1972 to that of 1973, we conclude that a figure of about 5½ percent represents the 1973 growth rate in real GNP compatible with the proposition that expansionary monetary and fiscal policies are inappropriate means of reducing the overall rate of unemployment below about 5 percent. Moderating our growth rate for the year to this extent can be accomplished by now only by reducing growth to appreciably below 5½ percent at an annual rate during the second half of 1973. The most recent preliminary growth figure available at the present writing—8 percent growth for real GNP (15 percent for money GNP) at an annual rate from the last quarter of 1972 to the first quarter of 1973—would in any event have been a strong warning signal of overexpansion. Meanwhile, policy makers have on their

---

[1] On the Phase II distortions see p. 153, below. At present the distortions caused by such controls, as well as the difficulties of enforcing the rulings, would be much greater because intense demand pressures have become much more general.

hands the additional problem of preventing a temporary price spurt from becoming embedded in the cost-structure and thereby perpetuating itself.

The Problem of Hardship Cases. As a result of the composition of unemployment, the difference in the number and weight of hardship cases between 5 percent unemployment and the conventional target rate of 4 percent is smaller than these two crude figures would suggest. Yet there *is* a difference, and it concerns directly the limited number of persons who have no serious unemployment difficulty at the very high activity levels we want to avoid but do have difficulty at the more reasonable levels for which we should be aiming. Observers who pretend to take a "tough" position on this problem, and to do so without qualifications, are apt to become suddenly "soft" when the most undesirable ways of alleviating hardships are smuggled into various programs. I have believed for some time that in a period when considerable savings could be had by pruning unsuccessful manpower programs and when many state and local governments are accumulating surpluses, a limited program of subsidized employment, mostly in nonprofit activities and partly combined with training, would be preferable to what appear to be the two major alternatives to such a program. These alternatives are (1) the subsidization of idleness and (2) monetary overexpansion combined with an inclination to experiment with wage and price controls even when demand pressures show in the markets. Since political considerations may push us into one of these two alternatives, I will add that I consider the subsidization of idleness in hardship cases a good deal *less* undesirable than overexpansion combined with a tendency to introduce and reintroduce controls.

The difficulty of dealing in a reasonable fashion with the difference in hardship cases arising at the 5 percent and the 4 percent level of overall unemployment is enlarged by two ill-conceived legislative measures, one of which is about to be phased out and the other of which is about to be introduced. The first of these, the Emergency Employment Program, was enacted at a time when the unemployment rate was in the neighborhood of 6 percent but was practically certain to decline in the near future. This program gave employment to persons without regard to whether the market economy would take care of them at the 5 percent rate. Indeed, a high proportion of those included had been unemployed for only a short time at the 6 percent level of unemployment. The second measure that will make matters more difficult is the impending increase in minimum wage rates, which will further increase the wage rigidities responsible for the coexistence of high unemployment rates in some labor categories with shortages in others.

Dangers to be Kept in Mind. Whatever second-best or third-best solutions are open in these circumstances for coping with structural manpower problems—problems of considerable significance—the main danger that faces us now is renewed acceleration of inflation *and* a serious recession in its aftermath. Avoidance of this danger requires clear awareness of the fact that, given the large changes in the composition of the labor force, a 5 percent overall unemployment rate, as computed by the now usual American procedure, has a different meaning today than it had, for example, in the mid-fifties or even earlier. If we consider the entire postwar period from 1947 to 1972, we find an average national unemployment rate of 4.7 percent—though for 1969, the peak year of an unsustainable inflationary expansion, the observed rate was ½ percentage point below the 4 percent "target," after which it rose to 6 percent during the recession. The average figure of 4.7 percent for the 1947 to 1972 period is, of course, much less influenced by changes in labor force composition than are data relating to recent periods.

Clear awareness is needed also of the fact that in the current sensitive phase of our expansion process we are faced, largely by bad luck, with price pressures originating in the area of primary products, and that the job of preventing the perpetuation of this initially temporary pressure requires, for the time being, all the more moderation in framing our monetary and fiscal policies. Hopefully even the first-year wage increases of 1973 will show a sense of responsibility, though the settlements will largely coincide with the manifestations of the temporary price pressures. Moreover, assuming no excessive monetary ease—but *only* on this assumption—first-year raises for a small fraction of the labor force should not set the tone for general money-wage trends in the future. Herein lie our hopes.

On the other hand, there exist two dangers, one that is probably minor and another that is major. The relatively minor danger is that even if we follow a policy of restraint from now on, enough of the temporary price spurt from the early part of the year will be built into the wage structure to make it impossible for producers to sell sufficient quantities of output at profitable prices later in the year when the lagged effects of the proposed policies of monetary restraint take hold. These lagged effects might lead early next year, or possibly even before the end of 1973, to no more than a minor cyclical setback against which in the given circumstances it is *not possible* to play *entirely* safe.

The greater danger is that, in an attempt to play safe against the possibility of a minor setback, excessively expansionary policies will be adopted—in which case the probability of highly inflationary cost trends will be greatly increased. Given the lags with which policies become effective, present expansionary measures would then continue to vindicate highly inflationary cost trends later this year. The ensuing spiral would eventually have to be stopped by measures causing a much more severe cyclical setback than one resulting merely from the inevitable minor oscillations around the growth trend. We have a choice: we can *risk* an early setback that is apt to be minor or we can head, with a small delay, for a much more severe recession.

Nature of the Study. In the main part of this study I shall explore in greater detail the problems sketched in the foregoing pages. After justifying my position on employment rate targets for expansionary policy, and after discussing the consequences of the present over-expansion, I shall turn to the question of available measures for redressing balance. Reasons will be given for focusing the discussion of these measures on monetary policy.

Manpower Problems: 1956-57, 1965, 1972

Why would it be very risky to employ expansionary policies for reducing our overall unemployment rate below about 5 percent? Let us review the period in which our inflationary troubles of the sixties started and compare that period with the present.

What had been a very mild rate of price increase started accelerating about 1965 and, by the end of the sixties, it forced our policy makers to step on the brakes consistently enough to allow a recession to develop. The policy line followed from 1965 to the closing years of the decade reduced the overall unemployment rate from 4.5 percent in 1965 to 3.5 percent in 1969 (and two decimals below that number in terms of lowest monthly data). The 3.5 percent overall rate for 1969 was 0.6 percentage points below the rate for 1956, in the year in which unemployment had fallen to within one decimal point of the conventional "target rate" of 4 percent. Presumably this target was defined with the labor-force composition of the mid-fifties in mind. Yet in 1969 the specific unemployment rates of various highly demanded labor categories were even further below their 1956 level proportionately than was the overall rate. Inflation kept steepening and the need to step on the brakes gradually became obvious, though it took some time before policy makers 'accepted the fact that it is a very difficult task to get an inflationary process of such duration and intensity under control. The process that has caused these difficulties originated in the conditions prevailing around 1965. It was fed by expansionary policies creating and further increasing the market tightness that became observable in the middle of the decade. In the present context, tightness of the labor market deserves considerable emphasis.

Comparison of 1965 and 1956-57. Whether we should say that inflation started accelerating "in an essential way" from the year 1965 to 1966 or from 1964 to 1965 depends on what we mean by "essential." Clearly noticeable acceleration of the price indices occurred in the transition from 1964 to 1965; but as measured by the consumer price index and the GNP deflator, inflation may nevertheless be said to have remained small until we started moving into 1966. A rate of increase of almost 3 percent in the consumer price index shows first when we move from 1965 to 1966, though a rate of increase somewhat in excess of 3 percent had already occurred in the wholesale price index in the transition from 1964 to 1965, largely as a result of rising food prices. On the other hand, the private nonfarm implicit deflator did not reach a rate of increase of about 3 percent until the transition from 1966 to 1967. It seems reasonable to summarize this by stating that accelerating inflation started to become bothersome about 1965. By the end of the decade the 3 percent yearly rate had been greatly exceeded by all "representative" price indices. For the consumer price index it had just about doubled.

At 4.5 percent in 1965, the overall "national" unemployment rate averaged 0.4 percentage points higher than in 1956 and 0.2 percentage points higher than in 1957. However, this does not mean that the labor market was less tight in 1965 than in the earlier two years. The essentials of the story cannot be told in terms of these overall rates. In 1965 the unemployment rate for *adult men*—aged 20 and over—was no higher than *3.2 percent*, less than the 3.4 percent rate observed for 1956 or the 3.6 percent observed for 1957, though in 1956 and 1957 we were said to be at about practical "full employment" with overall unemployment rates not significantly in excess of 4 percent. Further, in 1965 the unemployment rate for *married men* was down to *2.4 percent*, as compared to 2.6 percent in 1956 and 2.8 percent in 1957. In 1965 *white males aged 25 and over* had an unemployment rate of *2.5 percent*, three decimals lower than their 1956 rate. In interpreting these figures we must take into account the decline of the weight in the labor force of worker categories that have had below-average unemployment rates all along. We need to remember also that the differentials between the unemployment rates of some categories had risen (not including the black-white differential). These are the two changes that explain the fact that in 1965, as compared to 1956-57, a higher overall unemployment rate corresponded to the lower specific unemployment rates for various important worker categories listed above.

For example, in the nine years from 1956 to 1965, the weight of adult men in the labor force declined from 64 percent to 60 percent, and the weight of men of all races aged 25 and over declined from 60 percent to 54 percent. (It should be remembered that the age classes 20 to 24 have an appreciably higher unemployment rate than their elders.) In the same nine years, the weight of teenagers and of adult women rose from 36 percent to 40 percent. This rise is made up of a 2½ percentage point increase (from about 29½ to 32 percent) for adult women and a 1½ percentage point increase (from about 6½ to 8 percent) for teenagers. At the same time, whereas in 1956 the unemployment rate for adult women exceeded that for adult men by only 0.8 percentage points (the two rates in question were 4.2 and 3.4 percent), in 1965 the differential was 1.3 percentage points (4.5 versus 3.2 percent); comparing teenagers of both sexes with adult men, the percentage point differential had risen from 7.7 percentage points to 11.6 (the teenage rate was 11.1 percent in 1956 and 14.8 percent in 1965).

A very large proportion of the labor force had lower unemployment rates in 1965 than in 1956 and in 1957. This in itself does not provide a *definitive answer* to the question of how the tightness of the labor market in 1965 compares with its tightness in 1956 or in 1957. We should not go beyond saying that these data, viewed in isolation, do create a *presumption* that for a high proportion of the labor force—for highly demanded labor categories—the market was at least as tight in 1965 as in 1956-57. However, evidence provided by wage trends further strengthen this presumption, and does so very greatly.

From 1965 to 1966 the increase in compensation per man-hour accelerated significantly. This measure of the rise in hourly earnings (including fringes) accelerated from a rate consistent with very small price increases when productivity increases are normal to a rate of roughly 6 or 7 percent for 1965-66 (depending on whether we consider merely the private nonfarm sector or the private sector as a whole). Quite aside from the fact that for the period we are surveying the 6 and 7 percent range was not the peak, even these rates of increase corresponded to an inflation rate of more than 3 percent for long-run normal productivity increases in the private economy. Moreover, even if these rates of wage increase had not accelerated further, they would have corresponded to a rate of inflation very much in excess of 3 percent for the exceedingly small productivity increases recorded in the closing years of the decade both at "overstrained" resource-utilization levels and subsequently during the recession.

The chicken-and-egg problem involved in wage-price or price-wage escalation cannot be decided on the basis of these data or, to my knowledge, of any other. Accelerating price inflation and accelerating wage-cost trends established themselves at roughly the same time. It is true also that capacity-utilization rates in the manufacturing industries reached a very high level simultaneously—about 90 percent by the standards the Federal Reserve Board uses in collecting its utilization-rate data, and all along this appears to have meant *full* capacity utilization. But leaving the hopeless chicken-and-egg problem aside, the data do strongly suggest significant tightness of labor markets. An acceleration of the increase in compensation per man-hour from a rate falling short of 4 percent for 1964-65 to one in excess of 6 percent for 1965-66 is indicative of this tightness particularly because for the initial phase of steepening inflation the tightening is more clearly observable on wage-trend data for nonunionized than for unionized workers in the manufacturing industries.[2]

Were it not for these nonunion wage trends, we would have to rely largely on intuitive appraisals in rejecting the argument that in spite of what was said above—in spite of the low 1965 unemployment rate for adult males and for males 25 and over (particularly white males of those age classes)—the tightness in these specific categories during 1965 *could* conceivably have been less than in earlier years. After all, an internally consistent account of the matter *could* be put together in this fashion: (1) The likelihood that a worker finds a job which suits him and for which he is suitable rises with the worker's level of education. (2) If we compare years that are nearly a decade apart—such as 1956 or 1957 with 1965—we need to take account of rising education levels and, in particular, of the fact that in the later period, *pari passu* with rising education, a higher proportion of the

---

[2] See the data in Marten Estey, "Union and Nonunion Wage Changes, 1959-1972," in *Price and Wage Control: An Evaluation of Current Policies*, Hearings before the Joint Economic Committee, U.S. Congress, part 2, 1972.

prime-age male population was occupied in jobs typically associated with longer job tenure. (3) Therefore, in spite of the low specific unemployment rates for the most-demanded worker categories, the market for these workers *may* conceivably have been less tight than was the 1956-1957 market at the then existing practical full employment. (4) Price inflation and inflationary wage trends could, therefore, have developed merely because commodity markets became tight at the high capacity-utilization rates in 1965, and even though labor markets were not particularly strained, unions had sufficient market power to steepen money-wage trends significantly more-or-less simultaneously with the steepening of price trends.

Even on general grounds this may not be the most credible account of the initial phase of steepening inflation in the mid-sixties, but it is not necessarily an account one feels like rejecting *out of hand*. However, the nonunion wage trends of the early phase deprive this way of telling the story of whatever plausibility it may otherwise have. In the period beginning about 1965 wages clearly behaved as one would expect them to behave in a tight labor market.

Thus, as to the comparison of 1965 with 1956-57, the *correct* conclusion is suggested by placing the emphasis on the low 1965 specific unemployment rates of large and highly demanded worker categories. Little importance attaches to the qualification that the low specific rates of 1965—lower than those observed for 1956-57—*could* conceivably have reflected lesser tightness because of a negative correlation between unemployment and education.

When describing the 1965 adult male rate of 3 to 3½ percent, or the married male rate of about 2½ percent (and a similar rate for white males 25 and over), as "low" we must, of course, take account of the method by which unemployment rates are estimated in the United States. The method used is to interview someone found at home in a sample of households in order to learn the number of household members aged 16 years and over who have no work but have very recently been looking for work. Not only the "job losers" and the "job leavers" are included among the unemployed but also the new entrants and reentrants into the labor force, regardless of how short the duration of their unemployment may be.

Comparison of 1972 with Earlier Years. We have seen that the 4.5 percent overall unemployment rate of 1965 was in all probability associated with at least as much labor-market tightness as was associated with the smaller overall rates of 1956 or 1957. On similar grounds the available data create a strong presumption that at the end of 1972 when the overall unemployment rate was 5.1 percent, the labor market was only slightly less tight than in 1965. This is so in spite of the fact that, as we shall presently see, the specific rates for males observed for 1972 should probably be corrected upward to some extent in order to make them comparable with the rates for 1965 or earlier. The degree of tightness existing about 1965 played an important role in touching off accelerating inflation and hence *by the end of 1972 we arrived at a state that may be regarded as located near the danger zone.*

We note that in December 1972 (with seasonal correction) the adult male rate was 3.4 percent, the married male rate 2.4 percent, and the rate for white males 25 and over probably somewhat below this last figure. In 1965 these three rates were 3.2 percent, 2.4 percent, and 2.5 percent, respectively; in 1956 they were 3.4 percent, 2.6 percent and 2.8 percent. This would suggest roughly the same degree of tightness for December 1972 as for 1965 and at least the same degree of tightness for the end of 1972 as for 1956. However, the wording of the questions asked in the Census Bureau survey was changed somewhat in 1966 and it seems likely that the recent male rates should be corrected upward by a few decimal points to make them comparable with pre-1966 rates. In view of this it is preferable to conclude that by the end of 1972 we had arrived in the *neighborhood* rather than at the precise level of the labor-market tightness at which a serious inflation problem developed in the past. In terms of the overall unemployment rate the critical point may now be located slightly below 5 percent rather than slightly above that figure. At the end of 1972 we were slightly above that figure. On the other hand, the rapid rate of GNP growth in the first quarter of 1973 suggests that continued growth approximating that magnitude would reduce the unemployment rate well below 5 percent. Indeed by June 1973 the rate declined to 4.8 percent. This is occurring at a time when the danger exists that our "temporary" raw material price increases will be built into the wage and price structure with long-lasting effects, a danger justifying particular emphasis on demand-policy moderation.

At an overall unemployment rate of roughly 5 percent, there now exists, of course, more teenage and adult female unemployment than would have been the case in earlier periods. The representation of adult males in the labor force, which declined from 64 percent in 1956 to 60 percent in 1965 declined further to 56½ percent by 1972; the representation of adult women in the labor force, which rose from 29½ percent in 1956 to 32 percent in 1965, rose further to almost

34½ percent by 1972; and the representation of teenagers, which rose from 6½ percent in 1956 to 8 percent in 1965, rose further to 9½ percent by 1972.

Seasonally corrected data for the late part of 1972 indicate that at that time less than 40 percent of our unemployed were adult males; the remainder consisted of adult women (about one-third) and teenagers (almost 30 percent). Along with the significant increase in the representation of workers other than adult males in the labor force, the representation of those groups in the *employed part* of the labor force has also increased significantly. However, their proportionate representation has increased somewhat less in the employed part of the labor force than in the labor force as a whole and this reflects itself in a large increase in their representation in unemployment. The unemployed are a small fraction of the labor force. Hence a small discrepancy between a change in the proportionate representation in the labor force and a change in the representation in employment shows in a large change in the representation in unemployment.

This reasoning implies the realistic assumption that when it comes to appraising shortages, greater tightness in the adult male category and in certain of its subcategories should not be regarded as offset by the greater availability of other types of workers. In other words, at the end of 1972 the adult male rate of 3.4 percent and the married male rate of 2.4 percent should not be regarded as "offset" by a 5.1 percent unemployment rate for adult women and a 15.7 percent rate for teenagers (seasonally corrected). These worker categories are very imperfect substitutes of each other, and the unemployment differentials reflect in part at least the results of rigidities of the real wage structures.

As for the social problem involved in the higher unemployment rates of women and teenagers, we should remember that their unemployment is of shorter average duration than that of adult men. This is merely one of the reasons why fewer hardship cases are involved in female and teenage than in male (especially married male) unemployment. While, as was already said, there does remain a difference between the number and weight of hardship cases in a 5 percent as compared to a 4 percent unemployment economy, driving the economy into accelerating inflation is the least desirable way of coping with this aspect of the problem.

Inflation: Its Acceleration, Deceleration and Revived Acceleration

The preceding section examined some of the characteristics of the economy at the start of the strongly inflationary period in 1965. The characteristics were compared with those at the end of 1972 when, after years of steepening inflation and after the recession of 1970, the economy had returned to roughly the level of activity at which it was highly inadvisable to generate appreciable further cyclical expansion. By 1972 the rate of inflation had been greatly reduced—though subsequently serious pressures have emerged that hopefully will prove to be temporary. What were some of the salient features of the processes that took place *between* these dates?

Acceleration in the Sixties. During the five-year period, 1965-69, that ended with the onset of recession, the money stock denoted by M_1—defined as currency plus demand deposits—increased by 27½ percent. During the same period the money stock denoted by M_2—defined as M_1 plus time deposits at commercial banks (other than certificates of deposit in the value of $100,000 or more)—increased by 41½ percent. During this span there were only two years, 1966 and 1969, in which M_2 rose by less than about 8 percent and M_1 by less than 5 percent.

The first of these two years (1966) was the year of the temporary "credit crunch," a brief interlude which was shortly followed by a renewed significant increase in the money supply and, as we shall see, also by a year of significant fiscal deficit. After the very brief interlude of slow growth connected with the crunch of 1966, the inflationary expansion continued at a rapid rate. The second year in which the money supply rose little—M_2 merely by about 3 percent —did put an end to the cyclical expansion. That year (1969) ended with the cyclical downturn. To stimulate a recovery, monetary policy was significantly relaxed in the recession year of 1970; and during each of the recovery years, 1971 and 1972, M_2 rose by about 11 percent. (M_1 rose by 6½ percent in 1971 and by 8 percent in 1972.) The tightening of monetary policy prior to the recession resulted from the determination to end a cyclical phase that had led to steepening inflation; the degree of the subsequent easing of monetary policy, however, seemed to many of us to involve a serious risk of overexpansion.

Similarly the *reduction* of the fiscal deficit from 1967 (that is, from the first year in which the deficit was large) to 1968, and the subsequent accumulation of a fiscal surplus in 1969 resulted from an effort to fight inflation by a tax increase and by reducing the rate of increase in fiscal outlays. But the "stimulating" turnaround after the start of the recession was very large in the area of fiscal policy too.

Only quite recently has the President exerted a strong influence to slow the increase of government expenditures again.[3]

In the last year of the cyclical expansion that ended in November 1969—to be followed by a twelve-month recession, according to National Bureau dating—the overall unemployment rate was 3.5 percent, the specific rate for adult men about 2 percent, and that for married men about 1½ percent. The consumer price index, which prior to 1965 had been rising at a yearly rate of less than 2 percent, rose in 1969 by close to 6 percent (the peak annual rate of 6 percent was reached with a short lag in 1970, hence after the downturn). It was the intention of policy makers to reduce the inflation rate significantly without exposing the economy to anything worse than a mild and brief recession. The recession was in fact mild and brief. However, the recovery was slow in the first post-recession year (1971), leaving the overall unemployment rate in the neighborhood of 6 percent.

The recovery quickened significantly in 1972. While the yearly average unemployment rate for that year was still 5.6 percent, the monthly figure declined to 5.1 by December. Civilian employment rose by about 3 percent during 1972, reflecting partly the increase in the labor force age population, partly the increase in the civilian participation rate in the labor force, and partly a 0.9 percentage point decrease in the unemployment rate from December 1971 to December 1972 (the unemployment rate being always expressed in relation to the civilian labor force). The first quarter of 1973 brought the disconcertingly large (unsustainable) further rate of expansion on which we have already commented. We have also commented on the fact that special factors—raw material shortages—are in large part responsible for the renewal of heavy pressures on prices in 1973. The overexpansion in the first quarter of 1973 has made it much more difficult to cope with these pressures on the price level.

By 1972, before the recent price spurt started, the earlier policies aimed at greatly reducing the rate of inflation at satisfactory levels of business activity seemed to have borne fruit, though the administration's stated goals were not yet reached. It seems exceedingly unlikely to me that the relatively favorable price record of 1972—the year which ended with the unemployment rate down to only slightly

---

[3] The following were the national-income accounts surpluses, and deficits (minus sign), in billions of dollars for the successive calendar years. 1965: 1.2, 1966: −0.2, 1967: −12.4, 1968: −6.5, 1969: 8.1, 1970: −12.9, 1971: −21.7, 1972 (preliminary estimate): −18.1. The unified budget surpluses and deficits for the successive fiscal years were: 1965: −1.6, 1966: −3.8, 1967: −8.7, 1968: −25.2, 1969: 3.2, 1970: −2.8, 1971: −23.0, 1972: −23.2, 1973 (preliminary estimate): −17.8 (midyear budget review).

more than 5 percent—could have been achieved if the recession had been even milder or the recovery during 1971 faster. Diminishing the rate of inflation by a significant margin took time because inflationary expectations had become built into the decision-making process. The facts surveyed in the foregoing pages suggest that union power is unlikely to have played a major role in touching off the inflationary developments starting in 1965. It clearly did play a crucial role, however, in building inflationary expectations into the cost and price structure during the recession and the immediate post-recession period, when unemployment rates were in the neighborhood of 6 percent.

Deceleration during 1970-72. Much of the deceleration of price increases occurred not during the recession itself but after the upturn, in those phases of the recovery in which the overall unemployment rate was as yet significantly in excess of 5 percent and capacity-utilization rates were low. When the cyclical upturn occurred in November 1970 (by National Bureau dating), the rate of increase in the consumer price index had already slowed from its peak, but it was not yet clear to what extent the movements were merely erratic. By the first half of 1971 deceleration was clearly observable in the consumer price index: the rise was not much in excess of 4 percent at an annual rate.

But in the first half of 1971 the rate of increase of compensation per man-hour in the private nonfarm sector was still at about its highest level, that is, approximately 8 percent. Standard productivity increase (that is, the "normal" or long-run productivity increase by which producers are largely influenced) and the increase in the private nonfarm GNP deflator (slightly in excess of 4 percent) added up to appreciably less than this increase in compensation. Thus either the price increase had to accelerate again or wage increases had to decelerate. Some of us believed that market forces would respond to the low capacity-utilization rates and the high unemployment rates of 1971 by bringing about a deceleration of wage increases, not a renewed speed-up of price movements. We therefore saw no necessity for the introduction of direct price and wage controls. But this was highly controversial.

As we have seen, Phase I of a control program—the temporary wage and price freeze—*was* in fact introduced in August 1971. This was followed in November by Phase II, with prenotification requirements for large sellers and large employers intending to raise their prices or wages and with extensive arbitrary interferences into the price and wage structure. Only in January 1973 did Phase II give way to Phase III, which is focused specifically on a small number of areas, but retains the government's right to intervene also in other areas.

During 1972 the consumer price index rose by somewhat less than 3½ percent, the implicit GNP deflator rose by 3 percent (its nonfarm component by somewhat less than that but the fixed-weight counterpart of the GNP deflator by between 3½ and 4 percent), and compensation per man-hour in the private nonfarm sector rose by about 7 percent. It follows from the preceding that it is impossible to tell with assurance whether the controls deserve any credit either for the continuation of price deceleration up to 1972 or for a noticeable deceleration of increases in compensation per man-hour I continue to be very doubtful in this regard, and I continue to be impressed also by the fact that a good many illustrations (discussed in the footnote below) point to significant distortions caused by the controls.[4] Whatever one may think of the role of controls, in the late part of 1972 it appeared to make sense to express a favorable diagnosis of general economic trends by stating that inflation was greatly decelerated and unemployment reduced to the immediate neighborhood of 5 percent.

---

[4] In the *Wall Street Journal* (April 19, 1973), Assistant Secretary of the Treasury for Economic Affairs Edgar R. Fiedler gives an account of dislocations caused during Phase II of the control program (adding that such harmful consequences would show much more extensively in a period of generally strong demand than was the case at that time). (1) The lumber industry was faced with very active demand even then, and a considerable number of practices developed in that industry for unsubstantial further processing and the passing of products through a number of firms—partly even by fictitious transactions—in order to enable sellers to charge mark-ups (higher prices) in accordance with the state of the market. Nevertheless, the production of lumber products seems to have been held below the attainable level in order to avoid exceeding the permissible profit margins. (2) A number of complaints were heard from businessmen observing the wage regulations that their work force was being pirated by rivals. (3) The regulations made it less profitable for the petroleum industry to produce fuel oil than various other products, and this increased the fuel shortage last winter. We may add that price regulations *inevitably* have major distorting effects of this general type. (4) Soybean meal and phosphate fertilizers were fetching sufficiently profitable prices abroad to lead the producers of these products to give substantial preference to exports over domestic sales at regulated prices. (5) In a number of food and related industries (also in some others) there existed firms which could not raise their prices because as a result of an innovation they were selling some specific new product at a price that raised their overall profit margins to the permissible limit; for this reason at the prices which such firms had to set for their other products, their rivals producing only these other products could not have stayed in the market in the longer run. (6) Only with a substantial delay could the Pay Board and the Price Commission pass on cases which they had to decide, and the waiting lines were becoming increasingly long.

The Recent Revival of Acceleration. Yet some of us have had strong misgivings all along about the size of the momentum that monetary and fiscal policy was building into the system. The 8 percent annual growth rate in real GNP, along with a somewhat higher than 6 percent annual rate of increase in the implicit GNP deflator during the first quarter of 1973, justifies these misgivings in retrospect. It is true that the President took steps to keep fiscal expenditures from rising at the rate previously planned for 1973, and Chairman Arthur Burns of the Federal Reserve System declared repeatedly that 1973 would be a year of moderation in monetary policy. But the economy's expansionary momentum in the early part of 1973 suggests that it would have been much preferable to move in these directions earlier. It was the avowed objective of policy makers to create an environment in which the price trend performance of 1972 would not merely be repeated but would be somewhat further improved. Yet, under pressure from their opponents, they predicted that their policies would lead to a reduction of the general unemployment rate to well below 5 percent, and only belatedly did they shift to restraint. Nevertheless it may be argued that in the absence of further complications, a very limited period of overexpansion might not have created a serious problem. In fact, however, a further complication *has* developed. As things now stand, acceleration of inflation in the early part of 1973 is a fact that assumed dramatic proportions. The objective for 1973 should now be to bring about very significant deceleration in the course of the year, and gradually to get us back to where we would have been if specific complicating factors had not occurred and if policies of restraint had been adopted in time.

As for the specific complicating factors, the country had bad luck in that during 1972 a supply problem started overlapping with the problem of making it understood to the public that in the present setting demand-policies directed at the conventional employment rate targets were unrealistic. As a result of poor crops in many countries as well as of rising demand, the prices of agricultural products rose sharply and, for a while, the cost of living will continue to rise appreciably more than it did in 1972. During the year 1972 a mild manifestation of the short supply of farm products was observable in the fact that whereas the consumer price index rose by 3.4 percent, the food component of the index rose by 4.7 percent. As an indicator of what was in store this was a misleadingly mild manifestation of price pressures in the agricultural area, and more generally in the area of raw materials. The farm products component of the wholesale price index rose by more than 15 percent in 1972. Indeed, even the rise of the *general* wholesale price index (6.5 percent) compared very unfavorably with that of the consumer index, though this latter statement does not apply to the industrial-goods component of the wholesale index (which rose only by slightly more than 3.5 percent).

Subsequently the first quarter of 1973 brought very sharp increases in agricultural prices and in the general wholesale index, with the consumer index rising very steeply too. The first quarter's rise in the consumer price index was in excess of 8 percent at an annual rate, with the food component rising more than 25 percent, the non-food commodity component less than 5 percent and services less than 4 percent. The rise in the wholesale price index for the period was in excess of 20 percent at an annual rate, with its farm-products component increasing well in excess of 50 percent and even its industrial-products component somewhat more than 10 percent. From the last quarter of 1972 to the first quarter of 1973, the GNP deflator rose, as we have seen, by about 6 percent at an annual rate, this being true not only of the implicit deflator, which involves changing weights from quarter to quarter, but (roughly) also of the fixed-weight deflator. Regardless of how successful the policy makers may be in *keeping* "initially temporary" phenomena truly temporary, the price trend performance of 1972 will surely not be matched in 1973.

While it is very questionable whether the direct controls exerted any appreciable influence on the general price level, Phase II lasted long enough to lead to the "bulging" of some specific commodity prices after January 1973. This is a strictly short-run phenomenon, affecting goods and services the prices of which (and presumably the expenditures on which) had been kept artificially low in relation to other goods and services.

The significant specific price pressures in the agricultural area may lessen greatly or even end before the year is over. We are now relaxing our policies of acreage restriction and of governmental credit facilities to producers for keeping agricultural products in storage. Policy changes *were* introduced in these regards and they will contribute to the anticipated significant reduction of the specific farm-price pressures later this year. In addition, the large purchases of U.S. grain by the U.S.S.R. have in themselves played a significant role in producing this year's shortages in the United States. The huge size of these imports from the United States reflects Russian crop failures of unusual dimension. Nor was the U.S.S.R. the only country abroad that had an exceptionally bad crop last year. And, with respect to meat supply, domestically we seem to have been caught in the wrong phase of the "corn-hog" cycle. Furthermore, as was

155

already said, the impact on the domestic price level of the rise in foreign currency rates is also likely to be *partly* temporary, because in the longer run domestic products will be substituted for part of our imports.

The danger remains, however, that wage trends will react to the "temporary" worsening of the price trend, with long-run consequences. Furthermore, specific pressures on some prices—perhaps particularly on the prices of materials used in energy production (for example, oil and coal)—are apt to prove inherently long-lasting. To a limited extent a longer lasting adverse effect is likely to develop on the standard of living of all population groups, including wage earners. There is no reason to expect, however, that the long-run uptrend in living standards would thereby be seriously impaired.

Most of the specific adverse factors of 1973 are "inherently" temporary though it is difficult to predict to what extent it will be possible to avoid their perpetuation via labor cost increases. Understanding on the part of the union leaders would certainly help. After all, their recent experience shows that periods of rapid money-wage increases can easily become periods of very small real wage increases, as was the case in the late sixties. But at any rate we have here an additional reason for guarding against expansionary policies that would tighten the labor market to what would be the danger point *even* in the absence of these difficulties.

The Danger of Trusting the Hypothesis of "Inflationary Equilibrium" in Very Tight Labor Markets

The Inconclusiveness of Phillips-Curve Studies.

The analysis in this paper suggests that some unpopular decisions will have to be made if we are to avoid more than a temporary revival of accelerating inflation and a subsequent severe recession. Whenever conditions call for monetary-fiscal restraints, inevitably involving the risk—but by no means the certainty—of a relatively early setback, it is tempting to evade the issue by developing faith in the hypothesis of stable "Phillips trade-offs." These are allegedly stable trade-offs between inflation and rates of employment, even at very high employment levels. Were this hypothesis acceptable, we could conclude that even if expansionary policies produced very high degrees of labor-market tightness, the rate of price increases would become stabilized after a while. It would then be possible to gear the economy smoothly to the resulting steep inflation rate. However the underlying hypothesis is unsubstantiated, and it would be exceedingly risky to bet the country's fate on it.

Some econometric studies suggest the inflation rate can be *stabilized* at a high level even if policy makers are determined to keep the labor market very tight. Other econometric studies point more in the opposite direction. In earlier publications I have argued that the econometric models from which an answer to this question has been sought have led to wholly inconclusive results.[5] Considering the competence of the researchers who have put their minds to this type of exploration, it seems most unlikely that future econometric efforts can decide the question.

To express the difficulty briefly: several models do suggest that, after a period of transition, the inflation rate corresponding to a *constant* level of labor market tightness becomes stabilized, that is, there is a stable Phillips trade-off between inflation and labor-market tightness. According to these studies, the acceleration of the U.S. inflation in the second half of the sixties resulted from a significant *further tightening* of the labor market from year to year—not from a high degree of tightness per se—even though the official unemployment rate changed very little in those years. In other words, these models imply reliance on measures of labor market ease that are not identical with the official unemployment rate. The results depend entirely on what measures are selected. Yet at present there is no acceptable method for selecting the "appropriate" type and degree of correction of the official rate for deriving a "true" measure of labor market ease or tightness. Hence such inquiries, based on conflicting ideas about what the relevant variables are, have remained wholly inconclusive. It would, of course, be begging the question to make those corrections that yield a model with stable trade-offs.

Stable Trade-offs Limited to Ranges of Moderate Tightness. In general, it seems more promising to recognize here an obvious fact of economic-political life. The tighter the labor market, the more are employers (individually and in the aggregate) influenced by the risk of not being able to hire the workers they need to carry out their production plans. On the other hand, employers and unions realize that policy makers are, by implication, threatening them with imposing a penalty on increasingly inflationary cost and price tendencies.

---

[5] William Fellner, "Phillips-type Approach or Acceleration?" *Brookings Papers on Economic Activity*, 2: 1971 (Washington, D. C.: The Brookings Institution, 1971); *Case for Moderation in the Economic Recovery of 1971* (Washington, D. C.: American Enterprise Institute, 1971); *Aiming for a Sustainable Second Best During the Recovery from the 1970 Recession* (Washington, D. C.: American Enterprise Institute, 1971) and *Employment Policy at the Crossroads: An Interim Look at Pressures to be Resisted* (Washington, D. C.: American Enterprise Institute, 1972).

The penalty would be imposed by a policy not generating the effective demand needed for profitable operations if cost increases continued to accelerate. Individual employers and unions are aware of this implicit threat and know that other employers and unions are aware of it too. Hence market behavior is very likely to depend on which of two risks is weighted more heavily: the risk of *not being able to hire* the needed labor force *or* the risk of being caught in a situation in which *policy makers do not "vindicate" the costs* to which one has become committed.

This suggests that Phillips trade-offs are more likely to become stabilized—and, conversely, continuing acceleration up to the point where policy makers actually bring about a recession is more likely to be avoided—when labor-market tightness is moderate than when it is pronounced.[6] These considerations suggest also that the merely temporary character of acceleration, when an upswing is not allowed to carry the economy into high degrees of tightness, results partly from the fact that the policy makers' threat of forcing a recession becomes increasingly credible as the recovery moves into its advanced stages. Finally, this way of looking at the matter leads to the suggestion that policy makers should in any event try to avoid giving the impression that their anti-inflationary objectives are secondary. The slogan according to which full employment (in the sense of significant labor-market tightness) is more important than the avoidance of inflation misses the point. Policy makers guided by this slogan are apt to be buffeted from two directions: first, they are apt to get the economy into continually accelerating inflation and then, this being an intolerable condition in the longer run, they are likely to produce a significant amount of unemployment.

A specific variety of the argument for tolerating high inflationary pressures as a necessary price for very tight labor markets calls for introducing direct wage and price controls in high-pressure economies. These would allegedly improve the Phillips trade-offs. However, in the Western world administrative controls have consistently proved ineffective as means of suppressing intense demand pressures for more than a short period. Since even in the short run these measures are easier to circumvent for some products and services than for others, they have a strong tendency first to distort the allocation of resources and subsequently to expose the economy to a demand explosion. The experience of Western countries with direct controls applied in times of high demand pressure generally points

---

[6] In other words, a long-run Phillips function may be stable in ranges of moderate but not of high degrees of labor-market tightness.

in this direction—though their worth or worthlessness in our 6 percent unemployment economy of 1971 and of early 1972 may forever remain a controversial issue (as has been argued in detail earlier in this paper).

Even in Eastern European countries—which have exceedingly severe administrative sanctions for enforcement—it is readily observable that the maintenance of excess demand combined with direct controls greatly reduces the variety and quality of available goods and services. And regulated prices for items that become unavailable are, of course, not prices in the proper sense. The same observation applies to Western countries, except that in such circumstances in the West violations become much more frequent and, after a while, the controls are apt to be abolished.

With respect to comprehensive administrative controls—for example, the controls we had prior to the reduction in their scope in January 1973 (prior to Phase III)—the present danger is not so much that policy makers would be willing to accept a program of high permanent inflation with controls of indefinite duration. Rather, the danger is that they might reintroduce more extensive controls with the avowed objective of coping with the temporary difficulties of 1973. Considering, however, that the U.S. economy has moved into a period of demand pressures, this would nevertheless have the very harmful consequences discussed in this section. Even in a period of relatively slack demand the dislocations caused by the Phase II controls were far from negligible (see footnote 4 above). Furthermore, on-and-off comprehensive controls might well condition sellers of goods and services to generate large cost and price increases whenever the controls are off. This would lead to a highly undesirable, abrupt change in price tendencies and in the types of economic activity undertaken.

Money Supply Targets

What methods are available then for attempting to lead the temporarily overheated economy back to the neighborhood of its normal growth path? Which variables should our analysis of this problem place in the foreground?

The Present Need for Emphasizing the Money Supply. In the appendix to this study it is explained in detail why both the so-called neo-Keynesian and monetarist (quantity-theoretical) frameworks represent far-reaching simplifications of a generally acceptable analytical system. However, an appealing system to which general validity could be attributed would be far too unwieldy for application. We do not know enough about the relationships between economic variables to form a dependable judgment concerning the relative acceptability of alternative simplifying devices in any specific period. To some considerable extent the choice of a simplified framework for a specific purpose needs to be "played by ear," and even after the framework is chosen, adherence to the conclusions derived from it must not be unconditional. Nevertheless, with all these qualifications, a case can be made for applying a framework of monetarist character to the problem of redressing balance under the present circumstances of the American economy. On what considerations can that case be based?

First, given the political facts of life, our authorities have much more leeway in the near future for determining the money supply than for bringing about appreciable changes in the values of the fiscal variables. One may, of course, question the binding character of any political commitment not to raise tax rates, but tax revenues (federal, state and local) already correspond to about one-third of the GNP and to a higher proportion of the net product of the economy. At the present writing we may conjecture that the administration and our legislators are less firmly committed to the investment tax credit than to other elements of the tax structure. However, an off-and-on policy on this measure would lead to a degree of jerkiness in investment which would be inadvisable.

Second, during the period 1964-1969 interest rates rose sharply; the three-month Treasury bill rate, for example, rose from the 3 to 4 percent range into the 7 to 8 percent range. This period includes sub-periods in which the monetary authorities made deliberate but mostly unsuccessful efforts to prevent a continued rise in interest rates by making very large additions to the money supply. It is true, on the other hand, that some sub-periods of tight money brought a particularly steep rise in interest rates and that some sub-periods of easy money became associated with a reduction of the rates. Yet stepping up the increase in the supply of money during the second half of the sixties did *not* prove to be a dependable way of reducing interest rates or even of stemming their rise. Large increases in the money supply have inflationary consequences and, other things equal, a steepening of price expectations raises the money rate of interest at which lenders are willing to lend and borrowers to borrow. For the period under consideration, this argues against stressing the potential interest-reducing—hence velocity-reducing—effect of increased money supply; it argues *for* paying a good deal of attention to the link between the supply of money and the rate of money income.

Finally, it should be pointed out that in recent years rather simple numerical regularities have in fact been observable in the relationship between the increase in money supply and that of money GNP, though no one can say with confidence how much longer these regularities will persist. Indeed, these regularities do not apply to the current year in unmodified form.

Stability of Velocity over a Limited Period. The regularities in question have recently been discussed by Professor Milton Friedman in a semi-popular presentation published in the *Morgan Guaranty Survey* of February 1973. The essential regularity there relates to the ratio of money GNP in any quarter divided by the money stock two quarters earlier. Friedman used the M_2 measure of the money stock, that is, currency and demand deposits plus time deposits in commercial banks (other than large negotiable certificates of deposit).

Before taking a look at Friedman's recent findings, it might be useful to mention a regularity which shows—in the form in which I will describe it—only for the five most recent years. Although five years is a very short period of time, this regularity has the advantage of being a good and trendless relation between *changes* in M_2 and *changes* in money GNP for *yearly intervals*. The intervals are of the kind with which the recent report of the Council of Economic Advisers is concerned when trying to look into the future.

Calculate the percentage increase in M_2 from December of year t to December of year $t + 1$; calculate also the percentage increase in M_2 from December of year $t + 1$ to December of year $t + 2$. Compare the simple average of these two figures with the percentage increase in money GNP during (approximately) the second of these intervals, that is, from the last quarter of year $t + 1$ to the last quarter of year $t + 2$. For the past five years the difference between the average increase in M_2 and the increase in money GNP will be found never to exceed 0.9 percentage points, and to be negligible for 1972.[7]

The lag assumption implied in this procedure is, of course, a "blurred" one—short-run variations in the rates of change during the years are neglected. But the relevant lags *could* in fact lack sharpness or consistency, because while in economic life action is usually based in part on decisions made well ahead of time, these decisions can often be adjusted just before carrying them out. The

---

[7] The average deviation is about 0.6 percentage points.

relative significance of these two components of the decision-making process is unlikely to remain constant. At any rate I suggest that the foregoing numerical relation deserves to be kept in mind.

We now turn to Friedman's proposition concerning M_2 and money GNP. Employing the hypothesis of a definite (constant) two-quarter lag between the stock of M_2 and the current flow of money GNP, Friedman found that the ratio of these two magnitudes was highly stable for the eleven-year period 1962-72.[8] The mean value of the velocity so calculated—GNP at an annual rate divided by money stock—is 2.44 for the period, the highest value during the period being 2.50, the lowest 2.37. The standard deviation is merely 1.4 percent of 2.44.

To this statement on the small size of the standard deviation, however, a caveat needs to be added. Assume that—from one yearly period to another—M_2 rises by 10 percent (as has been roughly true in recent years). Assume also that Friedman's velocity term rises from 2.44 minus one-half of a standard deviation to 2.44 plus one-half of a standard deviation. Then the resulting underestimate of the change in GNP based on a velocity of 2.44 would be larger than the *maximum* error arising for the five most recent years when the crude relation previously discussed is employed. Nevertheless, the fact to be stressed here is that Friedman obtained a good relation for an eleven-year period, with an average velocity of 2.44 for M_2. (This number's reciprocal describes the money stock held per unit of yearly GNP; the ratio in question is 0.41.)

Concern in the present discussion with the M_2 aggregate, rather than with the money-stock aggregate M_1 defined as *excluding* time deposits, is supported also by exploratory work (with as yet tentative results) which Dr. Dan Larkins has undertaken at the American Enterprise Institute. For the period beginning in the first quarter of 1953 and going through 1970 this work points to a somewhat superior performance of M_2 in the context of the monetarist model used by the Federal Reserve Bank of St. Louis. However, the St. Louis model implies a trend for velocity, and the meaning of such a trend raises essential but unanswered questions. (When M_2 rather than M_1 is used in the St. Louis model, the trend in the *increase* in GNP in relation to the *increase* in money becomes statistically insignificant. But even for M_2 a trend in the velocity itself has been moving the velocity term *toward* the initially higher ratio of increase in GNP to increase in money stock.)

---

[8] To the appreciable increase in velocity in the early part of 1973 we shall return presently.

Regardless of whether we define money as M_1 or M_2, velocity has an uptrend with decreasing slope from 1948 to 1962. For M_1 this trend continues to the present. Only for M_2 does the trend become practically horizontal, that is, only for M_2 does it practically disappear—for the period 1962-72. Appropriately constructed models with the trend worked into them as a parameter are capable of relating the actual path of money GNP to monetary aggregates for much longer periods than the past five to eleven years. But such models become less convincing the less specific the explanation of the trend becomes. After all, a time trend becomes understandable only on grounds of an articulate hypothesis as to what is generating it.

Friedman belongs among those who do suggest a rational explanation. His explanation is not sufficiently specific, however, to permit policy makers to predict with reasonable confidence whether in the near future the velocity of M_2 will continue to be stable (or whether the velocity of M_1, which is de-emphasized in Friedman's reasoning, will continue to show a decelerating uptrend). Friedman, basing his conclusions partly on his and Anna Schwartz's work spanning a century of monetary history, suggests that "normally" velocity has a downward trend because, with rising real income and wealth, the public tends to afford itself the luxury of holding more money per unit of output. However, as a result of the inflationary tendencies of the postwar era—or rather of the public's gradually awakening awareness of these—a velocity-increasing effect developed which, in the postwar period, has outweighed the velocity-decreasing effect for M_1. For M_2 during recent years these two forces have just about balanced each other. Friedman suggests that, at rising standards of living, the velocity-decreasing effect of a relatively increasing demand for liquidity will sooner or later reassert itself on balance.

Reasonable as such suggestions concerning the factors causing nonlinear trends may be, one is tempted to look for a rule of thumb by which monetary policy can be guided in the immediate future without relying on vaguely explained trends. A tendency toward stability of the velocity of M_2 has now been observable for a number of years. A policy mindful of this fact—particularly of the relation between two-year averages of the growth of M_2 and the second year's increase of money GNP—would be moving in a framework that represents a far-reaching simplification of a generally acceptable system, sufficiently so to make "playing it by ear" at times inevitable.

Money Supply Targets. In trying to estimate the desirable 1973 rate of increase of *money GNP*, we make four jointly reasonable assumptions. With very little further *cyclical* expansion from the last quarter of 1972 to that of 1973 (with no cyclical reduction of the overall unemployment rate below about 5 percent), it is assumed first that the labor force would rise by 2 percent and second that output per man-hour in the economy as a whole would rise by 3 percent. Third, we assume that we may add to the resulting 5 percent real GNP growth ½ percent for a very small amount of cyclical expansion after the last quarter of 1972 at which time the unemployment rate was 5¼ percent. Fourth, we make a 5 percent allowance for the rise in the implicit GNP deflator for the year as a whole (a point to which I shall return presently). These four figures—2, 3, ½ and 5—add up to a 10½ percent increase in money GNP. On the assumption that the past regularities in the behavior of the velocity of M_2 will carry over into the unusual year 1973 the calculation *would* suggest for 1973 an increase of roughly 10 percent in M_2, only about 1 percentage point less than the 1972 increase. However, knowledge of the first-quarter increase of money GNP in 1973 and a guess concerning the subsequent increase strongly point to a velocity-increasing effect of the expectations generated by the unusually steep price trend of this period. We now have been obtaining a 2 to 4 percentage point increase in money GNP *in addition* to what could be expected on the basis of calculations of the foregoing type, and this suggests the desirability of keeping the 1973 increase in M_2 down to about 6 percent.

As for the inflation allowance made in our rough calculation—5 percent in terms of the implicit deflator for the year as a whole—this is greater than the allowance that would have been justified for 1972. We have seen that for the first half of 1973 a larger allowance will be required but the policies affecting the first half of this year are matters of the past. By using sufficient restraint from now on, policy should try to achieve the result that by the second half of the year further increases in the general price level should not be much steeper than they would have been if the temporary price spurt had not occurred. A rate of increase in the implicit GNP deflator by 5 percent during 1973 might imply a rise by less than 4 percent at annual rate during the second half of the year, though at the present writing the estimates for the first quarter of 1973 are merely pre-liminary and no second-quarter estimates are as yet available.

From the final quarter of 1972 to that of 1973 the growth in real GNP would then be about 5½ percent and the growth of money GNP about 10½ percent. Only for one or two quarters would this desirable course of events probably involve an annual real-GNP growth rate of less than the normal long-run rate of 4 to 4½ percent. This in itself would not imply a recession. However, an attempt to put the economy on the path suggested *would* soon lead to a setback if the cost trends that are developing should be steep enough to involve insufficient profitability for businesses unless the GNP deflator rises by considerably more than the inflation allowance made in our calculation. Given such cost trends the policy contemplated here would turn out not to have left sufficient room for the needed price increases on the quantity of output we have implied. *It is better to take this risk than to face the near certainty of a somewhat delayed but much more severe recession.*

Later, when hopefully we would be moving near our normal growth path and would not have started the year with 8 percent growth in real GNP, we should aim for real growth at a rate of somewhere between 4 and 4½ percent. With an inflation allowance of less than 3 percent, this would yield growth in money GNP at a rate of about 7 percent. The normal growth rate so described includes no allowance whatever for cyclical expansion, whereas a slight allowance for this was justified when we started from the last quarter of 1972. Nor does the normal growth rate include any accommodation for a post-recession catching up of labor force and productivity increases. Nowadays the "normal" growth of the labor force may be estimated at slightly less than 2 percent and that of man-hour output in the economy as a whole at close to 2½ percent.

Differential Hardship Cases in a 5 Percent versus a 4 Percent Unemployment Economy

At a more-or-less stabilized unemployment rate of 5 percent overall (as estimated by U.S. survey methods), the social hardship caused by unsuccessful job-seeking is smaller than most foreigners would infer from this figure. But there *is* a problem, compared with the hardships existing at 4 percent unemployment, and only through experimentation can we discover the least unattractive measures for coping with it.

For some time now I have been suggesting that it would be advisable (1) to arrive at an estimate of the *difference* between the number of persons with a long-term unemployment problem (because of long duration or frequent repetition) at a 5 percent overall rate and the number with such a problem at a 4 percent rate and (2) then to try to provide subsidized work opportunities mostly in nonprofit activities to a number of persons not exceeding this difference. This would, of course, turn out to be the difference between a fraction of

5 percent and an even smaller fraction of 4 percent. The program would imply selecting *up to the limit defined by this difference* the most suitable members of the labor force from among those who at a 5 percent overall rate are faced with a long-term unemployment problem involving hardships. The program would involve subsidized employment on a limited scale at a cost that could be covered by cutting various other manpower programs that have proved unpromising. The costs could in any event be partly borne by state and local governments whose financial situation is now enviable compared to that of the federal government. In the case of teenagers and some others, as well, the concept of subsidized *employment* might well shade over into that of subsidized *training*.

This way of reducing the overall unemployment rate to the neighborhood of 4½ percent would be much less damaging than reliance on further expansionary policies. Also, subsidized employment on a limited scale is preferable to subsidized idleness by means of "welfare"-type payments. However, even the latter is a distinctly less objectionable way to alleviate hardship than would be the effort (at best temporarily successful) to raise the employment rate to a high level by policies involving accelerating inflation.

Such a program of subsidized employment would have the desirable by-product of greatly reducing political pressures to carry expansionary policies too far. Some past and prospective legislative measures, however, have not improved the chances of agreement on such a reasonable course of action. In the introductory section of this paper—the Overview—it was pointed out that the lack of focus of the Emergency Employment Act led to experience which helped throw a bad light on programs of employment subsidization. And the impending increase of minimum wages will further increase the rigidities in the wage structure that are largely responsible for the coexistence of shortages in major labor categories with considerable unemployment in other categories. Whether for these reasons or others, policy makers' views on the problem of the limits of reasonable demand expansion do not seem to have crystallized. This, however, is a dangerous state of affairs. In practice uncrystallized attitudes—wavering—have led to undesirable consequences.

What are the main symptoms of this wavering which, given the political pressures, are perhaps understandable but must not be allowed to continue?

Gradually the public has been told by competent spokesmen of the government that, in the present circumstances, the 4 percent unemployment target is unrealistic and that the implications of any given overall unemployment rate are very different now than they were at the time when 4 percent was defined as the appropriate interim target and a 5 percent figure was considered much too high. What the public has been told in this regard is the truth. That it is the truth is borne out by the data set forth above about the various specific unemployment rates that correspond today to an overall rate of about 5 percent—the specific rate for married men and a good many other important specific rates. Policy makers have rightly stressed also that at present less than 40 percent of the unemployed consists of adult men, and very little more than one-half consists of workers who have either lost or left their jobs just before becoming unemployed (the others being new entrants or reentrants into the labor force). It has often been added that about half the total number of unemployed has been unemployed for less than five weeks, which is a fact of considerable importance even if it conveys no information about the number of spells of unemployment experienced in any year by those included in the count. Furthermore, when a family changes locations because of a more promising job for one of the spouses, it is often inevitable that the other spouse should have to look around for a while before finding suitable employment. This fact and the relatively high proportion of new entrants among women explain why women have a higher unemployment rate than men, as well as shorter average duration of unemployment. Higher than average unemployment rates for teenagers (a large proportion of whom are students) and for the age class 20 to 24 also have "legitimate" explanations.

All this is true and relevant to the problem. But it remains true also that more individuals suffer long-term joblessness in an economy with 5 percent unemployment than in one with 4 percent unemployment, and that this poses hardships for some whose interests policy makers will not in fact neglect. Any policy maker talking himself into the mood that he will persist in neglecting this aspect of the problem is insincere with himself.

Hence, while most official statements on employment policy emphasize the relatively small hardship component of the present rate of unemployment, it nevertheless is a fact that in the period in which excessive momentum was built into the economy most of them also expressed the judgment that enough expansion *should* and *would* be generated to reduce the overall unemployment rate well below 5 percent. A remarkable corollary to this, a giveaway as concerns a wavering condition of mind, is the emphasis of officials on the so-called full-employment budget—*with the implication that what really matters is the relationship between budgetary outlay and revenue at a 4 percent unemployment rate.* Such a position has a number of built-in contradictions. It is time to recognize clearly that the exercise of defining employment rate objectives without regard to the specific rates and then of trying to achieve ambitious goals by expansionary monetary and fiscal policy is practically certain to be a self-defeating way to deal with our social problems. This is a method leading, after a brief detour over a significantly inflationary period, to unnecessarily high unemployment levels, to insufficient profitability of investment, and to a low level of business activity.

It may not be too late to correct the overheating that has resulted from failure to develop a firm attitude to these matters. It may be too late to achieve this without *risking* a mild setback, but not too late to achieve it without causing a severe recession.

Conclusion

Some points bear repetition. Under pressure our policy makers have acted as if employment policy goals—mainly these goals—justified a degree of monetary-fiscal ease leading to overexpansion. Today, capacity utilization rates are very high in a large number of industries and unemployment rates for many important labor categories are near those observable in the mid-sixties when inflationary shortages started causing long-lasting trouble. Special difficulties originating in the raw materials sector—most of which will prove temporary *unless* they come to affect the trend in unit labor cost—have further complicated matters. Had it not been for these special difficulties and for the rapidity with which we have been moving, overexpansion would have become observable at a slightly later stage—but only slightly later.

Whether or not the policy of restraint advocated in this paper would lead to a cyclical setback early in 1974, or possibly even toward the end of 1973, cannot be predicted with assurance. It could avoid any noteworthy setback if awareness of the restraints among unions and employers prevented the perpetuation of "temporary" price pressures via steep wage trends. At any rate, a policy of ease—one that is willing to generate enough effective demand to finance the price trends corresponding to steeply inflationary cost trends at high activity levels—would involve very much more serious dangers. Such a policy would result in a somewhat delayed but all the more severe cyclical contraction.

Appendix: The Controversy about "Neo-Keynesianism" and "Monetarism"

A discussion of the effects of policies of expansion and of restraint needs to move in an analytical framework. For the purpose of the analysis presented in this study it made sense to use a framework placing a somewhat one-sided emphasis on the role of the money supply, though such a framework has major weaknesses as do all relatively simple tools which are readily usable in ad hoc policy making. These statements require clarification.

Any logically appealing general analytical framework is too complex to be employed when, in a situation such as the present, guidance is sought for prompt decisions. An appealing general framework would have to leave *a number of possibilities open*, in the sense of making the outcome in these regards dependent on a large number of variables about the effects of which not enough is known. For the present purpose three such possibilities will be distinguished. The second of these is of interest mainly because it needs to be understood "on the way to the third."

(1) In connection with the first possibility the *key statement* to be formulated is that the expansionary effect of an increased money supply on money income *may depend on whether the public's demand for money balances per unit of income increases merely slightly or very greatly when the money rate of interest is lowered*. If, for example, the monetary authorities increase the money stock by acquiring part of a given quantity of government securities, they thereby may lower the money rate of interest on these. The result will then be that the public will spend only *part* of its additional money on the acquisition of private securities and goods, because it will also increase its money-holdings per unit of income at the lower interest rates. At these lower rates liquidity is less costly; and having increased the weight of privately issued securities in their portfolios, the owners of assets will want to hold a larger quantity of money per unit of their income. By this reasoning we may conclude that even if the Federal Reserve increases the money supply by buying *privately* issued securities, interest rates on these will be lowered, the public will want to hold more money per unit of its income, and hence it will not increase its expenditures by the full money-equivalent of the securities that the monetary authority has removed from private ownership.

By the same type of reasoning we would conclude that if the government issues additional government securities and the money supply is not enlarged, interest rates will increase, and liquidity will become more costly. Having increased the weight of government securities in their portfolios, the owners of assets will want to hold a smaller quantity of money per unit of income at the higher interest rate. Hence fiscal policy may raise the total amount of expenditures—public plus private expenditures—for any given stock of money. So much for the "first possibility."

(2) In connection with the second possibility, to be explored mainly to prepare the ground for the third, the *key statement* is that the expansionary effect of an increased money supply on money income *may not depend importantly on how the public's demand for money balances per unit of income is influenced by changes in the money rate of interest.*

We now consider the possibility that the interest-rate effects of money-creating operations of the Federal Reserve (or the interest-effects of the Treasury's security floatings) last only for a short transition period during which the public decides what to buy with the additional money it has acquired (or what purchases to forgo because of having spent more money on government securities). If government securities are removed from the public's portfolio by means of the money-creating operations of the Federal Reserve, the amounts that the public obtains for these securities will be fully spent for privately issued securities and for commodities. Money-creating activities of the Federal Reserve by means of the purchase of privately issued securities would also lead with a short lag to the purchase of an equivalent quantity of newly issued securities and additional goods. This is *not* because the public's demand for money per unit of its income *would* remain unaffected by changes in the money rate of interest but rather because, given the public's price expectations, the money rate of interest *does not change*. The money rate does not depend on the supply of money (except for an interest-rate effect during a brief period of transition). Assuming given price expectations—an assumption that will be relaxed in the discussion of our third possibility—and disregarding a brief period of transition during which the interest rate *is* influenced by changes in the money supply, the rate is determined by the productivity of investment.

For this same reason the issuance of additional government securities at a given money supply will not raise the money rate of interest for more than a brief transition period. Hence this policy will result not in decreased money holdings per unit of income but in lesser outlays on private securities and on goods. The sum of government and of private spending will remain unchanged, given the money supply.

The conclusion under our second possibility is that, by increasing the money supply, we may bring about an increase in money income at a constant money rate of interest, and without changing the ratio of the increased money stock to spending and to income. Fiscal operations that are not supplemented by monetary operations will, on the other hand, have no important effect on total spending and income, except during a transition period. If fiscal operations *are* supplemented by changes in the money supply, then the observed results—except those of a relatively brief period of transition—are attributable to the monetary and not to the fiscal part of the joint operation. So much for the second possibility.

(3) Thirdly, the possibility exists that the propositions in (2), including the italicized *key statement*, prove valid with the *addition and modification* to be expressed in (a) and (b):

(a) What is determined by the productivity of investment and what, aside from a brief transition period, remains unaffected by a change in the money supply is not the money rate but the *real rate of interest*, obtained by deducting from the money rate the expected rate of price increase (or adding the expected rate of price decrease).

(b) By increasing the supply of money, policy makers may well *steepen* inflationary expectations—thereby raising money expenditures all the more. In view of (a), this implies that expansionary monetary policy may well *raise* the money rate of interest. This, of course, is in particularly sharp contrast to the first of our three possibilities.

In all three cases, it should be borne in mind that an increase in the money supply is apt to become associated with a smaller increase in real income (or output) than in money income, because of the increase in the price level occurring when money income expands. Furthermore, it should be added that, in the event of fixed exchange rates, none of these possibilities have much relevance to a *small* and *open* economy. This is true because if the money supply is increased in such an economy alone, then most of the addition to the supply flows over into other economies at an approximately unchanging money rate of interest. But the United States has, of course, a very large economy. And it does not at present have fixed exchange rates.

An analytical framework claiming "general validity" should allow for all three possibilities set forth above. If we had sufficient knowledge of the workings of our economies, we should be able to relate the probability of these alternative outcomes to specified economic variables. The present state of knowledge is insufficient for handing to policy makers a useful formal model of this sort.

Hence, after a largely intuitive or "casual" appraisal of various factors, we need to *simplify* the analysis by placing the emphasis on one or the other of these possibilities.

The framework usually labelled neo-Keynesian and that usually described as quantity-theoretical (sometimes also as "monetarist") represent such simplifications. *The neo-Keynesian simplification places the emphasis on the first of our three possibilities and the quantity-theoretical on the second or the third, mostly attributing considerable importance to the third possibility.* It follows that a general analytical system that would allow for all three possibilities can be obtained by introducing additional elements *either* into a so-called neo-Keynesian *or* into a quantity-theoretical (monetarist) framework. A system thus obtained could not legitimately carry either of these labels. Indeed, it is questionable how good these conventional labels are even for describing the simplified frameworks, but in this regard it seems best to follow the ruling conventions.

An explanation is given in the text of why, for the specific purpose of this analysis, it seemed appropriate to bear primarily the second and the third possibilities in mind.

Cover and book design: Pat Taylor